# Writing the Right Word

# Writing the Right Word

## "Its Effect Can Affect Your Writing"

*Dave Dowling*

Writers Club Press
San Jose New York Lincoln Shanghai

**Writing the Right Word**
**"Its Effect Can Affect Your Writing"**



Writers Club Press
an imprint of iUniverse, Inc.

For information address:
iUniverse, Inc.
5220 S. 16th St., Suite 200
Lincoln, NE 68512
www.iuniverse.com

ISBN: 0-595-20830-4

Printed in the United States of America

*To Mary and Tim*

*"The difference between the almost right word and the right word is really a large matter- 'tis the difference between the lightning-bug and the lightning."* — Mark Twain

# Preface

Unlike math and science, writing has very few absolutes. To that end, we're faced with making choices, and many times those choices are word choices. Since I began teaching technical and business writing in industry years ago, one lesson never grew old—an exercise on when to write the right word. Many writers confuse *complement* when they mean *compliment*, *compose* when they mean *comprise*, or *assume* when they mean *presume*. And hundreds of other mistaken word identities also exist. This quick reference aims to filter this confusion of words. Remember, writing is much easier to comprehend when the noise around it is eliminated.

Though totally not inclusive of all word pair mistakes, this book speaks to many of the common word choices that challenge us daily. It consists of more than 600 entries and the meanings of more than 1,500 individual words. Much of the content is based on word problems I've witnessed during my 25 years of technical and business writing.

If you're looking for the basic homonyms such as *to*, *too*, and *two*, or *here* and *hear*, you won't find them here. But you will find the basic pronoun possessives (*their*, *they're*, *there*, *who's* and *whose*, and *you're* and *your*) because they still give us problems. I've tried to eliminate obvious synonyms and include just word pairs where the word distinction is still important yet challenging.

Note that a few entries may seem trivial and others may seem a bit obscure or obsolete. But overall you'll find it a good mix of problem words (*among* vs. *between*, *flounder* vs. *founder*, *blatant* vs. *flagrant*). Also included are a few notes on phrases that often lead to problem writing (*between you and I*, *one of the only*, and others), and a few common redundant abbreviations (*ATM machine*, *PIN number*, and others).

For each entry in this reference, the difference between the words is explained, and in most cases, a simple sentence example showing the correct usage is provided. The word definitions provided are intended strictly as aids and not dictionary definitions. They should help you differentiate between the words. Current dictionaries, popular writing books, and reputable style guides were among the many resources consulted for this book. The word list is arranged alphabetically according to the first word in the set.

In addition to this reference, keep a current dictionary, thesaurus, and grammar book handy to guide all your writing and editing. And refer to those resources as well whenever you doubt the appropriateness of a word or phrase.

Always think about the words you use. Accuracy in word choice is a key to effective communication. In your daily writing, try to make sure you apply the *right word* for the *right meaning*. By doing so, its effect can affect your writing in a positive way.

*Dave Dowling*

*Owego, New York*

# Acknowledgements

This book would not have materialized without the sincere encouragement of my friend and former co-worker, Harry Dracon. After reading my weekly "Writing the Right Word" articles on the company's intranet site, Harry strongly urged me to expand this idea into a book. I was reluctant at first because I doubted an audience existed for such a topic. I was wrong, and today I'm certainly glad I listened to a friend. Thank you, Harry, for all your inspiration, belief, and support. You were right to push me in this right word direction.

Whether it was ideas, constructive criticism, or encouragement when this project was in its online infancy, I must thank a few other people who influenced me on this word journey. I'm particularly grateful to Douglas Cavanaugh, Valerie Haas, Eric Hards, Harold Sasnowitz, and Lois Totten for all their professional advice and expertise. Thanks, friends, for your generous time, and thanks for being there.

And a special thanks to Bruce Roberts who generously offered to use his word-processing pencil to edit these pages. Thanks Bruce for your expert editorial advice. You're a pro who knows prose.

Finally, a heartfelt thanks goes to my wife Mary and son Tim. Without their help, belief, and reassurance, this book would not exist. They're my best critics, my best friends, and the joy in my life.

# A

*"By words the mind is excited and the spirit elated."* — Aristophanes

## A, an

**A** and **an** are *indefinite* articles.

Use **a** only before a word beginning with a consonant sound.
*A one-way street* (The *o* in *one* is a vowel, but the first sound is *w*, a consonant sound.)
*A submarine* (The *s* is a consonant sound.)
*A yellow flower* (Initial *y* is a consonant sound.)

Use **an** only before a word beginning with a vowel sound.
*An apple* (vowel sound of short *a*)
*An igloo* (vowel sound of short *i*)
*An entrance* (vowel sound of short *e*)

Note: Use **a** before a pronounced or aspirated *h* (**a** historian, **a** house, **a** hotel). Use **an** before a silent *h* (**an** heir, **an** honor, **an** hour).

## A ways

Incorrect phrase. The article **a** is singular; therefore, the word following **a** must also be singular (**way**).
*The Town Square Mall is **a** little **way** down the parkway.*

## Abdicate, abrogate

**Abdicate** means to give up, relinquish power, or renounce formally.
*By leaving the job, did Paul* ***abdicate*** *his rights to a vested pension?*

**Abrogate** means to abolish, cancel, or revoke something.
*Why are the Washington politicians seeking to* ***abrogate*** *the treaty?*

## Ability, capacity

**Ability** refers to the power or quality to do something.
*Some vitamins are said to have the* ***ability*** *to prevent colds.*

**Capacity** refers to the ability to hold or contain something.
*Madison Square Garden has a* ***capacity*** *of more than 20,000 seats.*

## Abjure, adjure

**Abjure** means to recant, renounce, or repudiate something.
*He* ***abjures*** *all rights to his citizenship.*

**Adjure** means to appeal, entreat, or order something.
*The minister* ***adjured*** *the congregation to be quiet.*

## Abnormal, subnormal

**Abnormal** means deviating from the average.
*Joyce's* ***abnormal*** *powers of concentration enables her to score well.*

**Subnormal** means less than normal or below the average.
*His SAT scores are* ***subnormal*** *and not as high as he expected.*

## About, approximately

**About** refers to a rough estimate.
*We are **about** halfway through the class and enjoying every minute.*

**Approximately** refers to near accuracy.
*The college currently enrolls **approximately** 4,000 students.*

## ABS braking system

Redundancy. ABS means *Anti-lock Braking System*. Just use ABS.

## Abstemious, abstinent

**Abstemious** means eating or drinking in moderation.
*Barb's **abstemious** habits probably ensures her a longer life.*

**Abstinent** means abstaining from something (food, drink, and so forth).
*The young group pledges to remain **abstinent** until the legal age.*

## Abstractedly, abstractly

**Abstractedly** means not paying attention, preoccupied, or removed.
*He sat through the entire lecture gazing **abstractedly** out the window.*

**Abstractly** means difficult to understand, not concrete, or unspecific.
*Without real pictures, she could just **abstractly** describe the invention.*

## Abstruse, obtuse

**Abstruse** means complex, deep, or difficult to understand.
*To the average person, Einstein's theory of relativity is **abstruse.***

**Obtuse** means dull witted, not too sharp, or slow to understand.
*I apologize if I am being **obtuse**, but I still do not understand the point.*

## AC current

Redundancy. AC means *Alternating Current*. Just use AC.

## Accede, concede, exceed

**Accede** means to take a position of authority or yield.
*She may **accede** to the throne, but only after taking the required oath.*
*I **accede** to your demands, as long as the requirements are realistic.*

**Concede** means to accept reluctantly.
*Some voters urged the candidate not to **concede** on election night.*

**Exceed** means to surpass.
*The product and service **exceed** our customer's expectations.*

## Accept, except

**Accept** as a verb means to admit, receive, or agree with something.
*I **accept** him to our organization with pleasure.*
*We **accept** your invitation to the ceremonies with gratitude.*
*They **accept** the jury's verdict with no problem.*

**Except** as a preposition means other than.
*Mary's grades are satisfactory in every subject* ***except*** *science.*

**Except** as a verb means to leave out or exclude.
*If you* ***except*** *his freshman grades, Ryan has an impressive average.*

## Access, excess

**Access** refers to an increase, outburst, or permission.
*Their winnings at the casino gave them an* ***access*** *of wealth.*
*What started as a small dispute suddenly turned into an* ***access*** *of rage.*
*We gave the users* ***access*** *to the secured web site.*

**Excess** refers to overindulgence or surplus.
*John and Betty have an* ***excess*** *of property they would like to sell.*
*At last summer's company picnic, a few employees ate to* ***excess****.*

## Accessary, accessory

**Accessory** is the preferred spelling, but either one is acceptable.

## Accessible, assessable

**Accessible** means capable of being approached, influenced, obtained, or understood.
*She works for an* ***accessible*** *supervisor whom everyone likes.*
*"Minds* ***accessible*** *to reason."* - Thomas Macaulay
*He develops technologies to make TV more* ***accessible*** *for the disabled.*
*The information is readily* ***accessible*** *to a nontechnical audience.*

**Assessable** means capable of being evaluated.
*Every 2 years the* ***assessor*** *classifies every item of assessable property.*

## Accident, incident, mishap

**Accident** refers to an unforeseen or unplanned event (good or bad).
*George's call about the job opening is just a lucky* ***accident****.*
*The 1986 Chernobyl* ***accident*** *was due in part to a flawed reactor design.*

**Incident** refers to a minor or simple occurrence (good or bad).
*The entire* ***incident****, which took place over 2 days, was recorded.*

**Mishap** refers to a minor unfortunate occurrence.
*Though no one was hurt, a* ***mishap*** *occurred during the celebration.*

## Accidentally, accidently

**Accidentally** is the preferred spelling, but either one is acceptable.
*If you* ***accidentally*** *delete the file, it is possible to restore it.*

## Acclamation, acclimation

**Acclamation** refers to an oral vote or praise of some kind.
*The members passed by* ***acclamation*** *a motion to start a relief fund.*
*The Honor Society appreciated the* ***acclamation*** *of the principal.*

**Acclimation** refers to adapting to a new climate, environment, and so on.
*Karen's* ***acclimation*** *to the new climate took longer than she had expected.*

## Accord, accordance

**Accord** refers to an agreement or settlement with something.
*Congress arrived at a unanimous* ***accord*** *on constitutional amendments.*

**Accordance** refers to the conformity or following of something.
*The guideline is in **accordance** with the Stock Exchange Regulations.*

## Accuse, allege

**Accuse** means to blame or charge someone with wrongdoing.
*No one among his classmates **accuses** him of doing anything wrong.*

**Allege** means to claim something not yet proven.
*The investigator **alleges** the investors were tricked by a huge scam.*

## Acetic, aesthetic, ascetic

**Acetic** refers to things having an acid characteristic.
*Because of its **acetic** taste, there's a good chance the juice is old.*

**Aesthetic** refers to artistic or beautiful things.
*The architect designs churches with **aesthetic** considerations in mind.*

**Ascetic** refers to a person who is austere in appearance, manner, or attitude.
*He lives an **ascetic** existence, supporting himself modestly as a farmer.*

## Acknowledgment, acknowledgement

**Acknowledgment** without the *e* is preferred in American usage.
*Applicants are now receiving **acknowledgment** letters from the office.*

## Acme, climax

**Acme** refers to the highest point.
*To his credit, Ed's performance was the **acme** of the piano recital.*

**Climax** refers to the point of greatest intensity in a series of events.
*The **climax** of the night's events is the fireworks' display.*

## Acquaintance, friend

An **acquaintance** is a person one knows. A **friend** is a person one knows, likes, and trusts.
*Joe is a good example of an **acquaintance** who became a close **friend**.*

## Acquiesce in, acquiesce to, acquiesce with

**Acquiesce** means to consent or comply without protest. When **acquiesce** takes a preposition, it is usually used with **in**.
*Their government cannot **acquiesce in** the occupation of that country.*

**Acquiesce** and the preposition **to** is less common, but also acceptable.
*Gracie, Audrey, and Patrick **acquiesced to** their parents' wishes.*

**Acquiesced with** is considered obsolete.

## Acquitted from, acquitted of

**Acquitted of** is the preferred phrase.
*The suspect is **acquitted of** all charges relating to the espionage case.*

## Acute, chronic

Concerning physical condition:

**Acute** refers to an extremely severe or sharp condition.
*While playing basketball today, Bob experienced **acute** stomach pain.*

**Chronic** refers to a lingering or prolonged condition.
*Jim unfortunately suffers from severe* ***chronic*** *lower back pain.*

## Ad, add

**Ad** is the shortened form of **ad**vertisement.
*We placed an* ***ad*** *in the classified section of Sunday's paper.*

**Add** means to total something.
*If we* ***add*** *all our golf scores, we scored much better than many teams.*

## Adapt, adept, adopt

**Adapt** means to adjust, change, or make suitable.
*Christian* ***adapts*** *well to new working environments.*

**Adept** means to be skilled.
*Francis is* ***adept*** *at shuffling and dealing cards.*

**Adopt** means to accept or to take as your own.
*Because of its merits, we shall* ***adopt*** *your proposal immediately.*
*We* ***adopted*** *our son Timothy 10 weeks after his birth.*

## Addenda, agenda

**Addenda** is an addition to something.
*The* ***addenda*** *to the manual describes the new hardware requirement.*

**Agenda** is a list of things to do.
*The* ***agenda*** *for this year's conference is quite interesting and varied.*

## Adduce, deduce, deduct

**Adduce** means to cite as an example or proof in an argument.
*The attorneys made no attempt to* ***adduce*** *fresh evidence in the case.*

**Deduce** means to conclude from a general rule, principle, or reasoning.
*The class* ***deduced*** *from the laws of physics that the plane would not fly.*

**Deduct** means to take away from a total or a quantity.
*Some people believe too many taxes are* ***deducted*** *from their wages.*

## Adhere, cohere

**Adhere** means to stick fast, to remain devoted, or to carry out a plan.
*The wallpaper should* ***adhere*** *to the wall quickly.*
*They have* ***adhered*** *to that particular faith for many years.*
*We are taking your advice and* ***adhering*** *to the revised plan.*

**Cohere** means to stick or hold together as part of the same thing.
*Generally, the film fails to* ***cohere*** *with the events in the book.*

## Adherence, adherents

**Adherence** refers to faithful commitment.
*His* ***adherence*** *to the corporation's quality goals was never in doubt.*

**Adherents** refers to advocates or supporters.
*The House passed legislation that pleased* ***adherents*** *of tax reform.*

## Adieu, ado

**Adieu** means goodbye.
*Since joining the health club, they bid **adieu** to bad eating habits.*

**Ado** means bother, fuss, or trouble.
*"Husband, let's follow to see the end of this **ado**."*
— "The Taming of the Shrew"

## Adjacent, adjoining

**Adjacent** means next to something without making physical contact.
*The basketball arena is directly **adjacent** to the team's hotel.*

**Adjoining** means a common point of contact.
*The basketball team also has **adjoining** rooms in the hotel.*

## Adjudicate, arbitrate, mediate

**Adjudicate** means to act as a judge in certain disputes.
*The department has jurisdiction to **adjudicate** all of the appeals.*

**Arbitrate** means to be neutral in a judgment.
*Ken willingly agrees to **arbitrate** the contract dispute for the two parties.*

**Mediate** means to bring parties together or reconcile differences.
*Sandy is attempting to **mediate** the differences between the two children.*

## Adverse, averse

**Adverse** means difficult or unfavorable (usually related to things).
*The proposal could have an **adverse** effect on our overseas business.*

**Averse** means strongly opposed (usually related to actions or people).
*The new public relations director is **averse** to our business proposal.*

## Adversity, diversity

**Adversity** refers to affliction, hardship, or misfortune.
*After a year of financial **adversity**, the young company rebounded well.*

**Diversity** refers to an assortment or a variety of things.
*Overseas investments certainly add **diversity** to William's portfolio.*

## Advert, avert

**Advert** means to call attention to or refer to something.
*The speaker **adverted** to an earlier point Kelly made at the meeting.*

**Avert** means to turn away or ward off something.
*To avoid any schedule slips, the workers would like to **avert** a strike.*

## Advisedly, intentionally

**Advisedly** means deliberately or with careful consideration.
*The spokeswoman chose her words to the media carefully and **advisedly**.*

**Intentionally** means with intent or purpose.
*The author **intentionally** writes the stories for younger audiences.*

## Adviser, advisor

**Adviser** is the preferred spelling, but either one is acceptable.

## Aerie, airy, eerie

**Aerie** means nest.
*Have you ever been to the mountains and seen an eagle's **aerie**?*

**Airy** means breezy.
*The **airy** conditions at the New Jersey shore always keep us cool.*

**Eerie** means spooky.
*The séance we attended was an **eerie** experience for everybody.*

## Affect, effect

The verb **affect** generally means to influence or cause change.
*The moon and sun can **affect** the ocean's tides.*

The verb **effect**, less common, means to bring about or accomplish.
*The new CEO **effected** just a few changes to their company.*

The noun **effect** generally means result.
*Carbon dioxide is the biggest contributor to the greenhouse **effect**.*

Memory hook: If you **affect** something, you can have an **effect** on it.

## Affectation, affection

**Affectation** refers to artificial, exaggerated, or false behavior.
*Forget the vocabulary **affectations**. We prefer just plain language.*

**Affection** refers to fondness toward someone.
*The neighborhood has a deep **affection** and respect toward that family.*

## Affinity, eternity, infinity

**Affinity** means a close relationship or connection.
*The organization has a strong **affinity** toward environmental issues.*

**Eternity** means unending time or forever.
*His long speech at last year's convention seemed like an **eternity**.*

**Infinity** means unlimited quantity, space, or time.
*From the ground, that highway appears to go on for an **infinity**.*

## Afflict, inflict

**Afflict** means to inflict suffering upon someone or something.
*The disease first **afflicted** people who were not vaccinated.*

**Inflict** means to cause by an aggressive action.
*The truck hit a parked car and **inflicted** severe damages to it.*

## Affluent, effluent

**Affluent** refers to the rich or wealthy.
*Joan jokingly claims she is from an **affluent** background.*

**Effluent** refers to a river, stream, or lake that flows out.
*The farmer uses water from a nearby **effluent** to water his garden.*

## Afterward, afterwards

**Afterward** is preferred in American usage.

## Aggravate, irritate

**Aggravate** means to make worse or more severe.
*Research shows that gum disease can **aggravate** chronic lung problems.*

**Irritate** means to annoy or make more sensitive.
*We can think of a few things that **irritate** us about his management style.*
*Vitamin C, aspirin, iron, and potassium can all **irritate** the esophagus.*

## Agree to, agree with

**Agree to** means consent to something.
*We hope Congress can **agree to** a compromise this year.*

**Agree with** means to be in accord with something.
*Both parties **agree with** each other on the new spending plan.*

## Aid, aide

**Aid** refers to assistance.
*Animal **Aid** is one of the oldest animal rights groups in the world.*

**Aide** refers to a helper.
*The congressional **aide** says the Senator is unavailable for comment.*

## Aisle, isle

**Aisle** refers to a passageway between seats, traffic, and other things.
*Two by two the wedding party marched down the **aisle**.*

**Isle** refers to a small island.
*The **Isle** of Wright was a famous 1970's concert venue in England.*

## All ready, already

**All ready** means totally prepared.
*Steve tells us the system is **all ready** and available to use.*

**Already** means by this time or so soon.
*It was **already** noon before Steve could get the system to restart.*
*Why are you stopping the system **already**?*

## All right, alright

**All right** is always two words. **Alright** is considered a nonstandard word. Avoid its use.
*It's **all right** to be nervous before an important speech.*

## All together, altogether

**All together** means in one complete group.
*The quarterly reports are **all together** on the conference room table.*

**Altogether** means completely, entirely, or totally.
*The presentation is **altogether** too long for next week's meeting.*

## All ways, always

**All ways** means by every way or method.
*Please look **all ways** before crossing that busy intersection.*

**Always** means all the time or forever.
*We **always** remember the good things Chris and Jim did for the poor.*

## Allay, alleviate

**Allay** means to make it less or to delete altogether.
*The government sought to **allay** the oil shortage fears.*

**Alleviate** means to relieve something unpleasant or painful.
*The aspirin should soon **alleviate** some of your discomfort.*

## Allot, alot, a lot

**Allot** means to allocate or share.
*The education budget **allots** money for many new reading programs.*

**Alot** is not a word.

**A lot** is always two words.
***A lot** of people today are doing business by way of the Internet.*

## Allude, elude, refer

**Allude** means hinting or referring to indirectly.
*The memo did **allude** to past equipment failures and problems.*

**Elude** means to avoid or escape.
*The base runner tried to* ***elude*** *the shortstop's tag.*

**Refer** means to make direct reference to something.
*We should* ***refer*** *to the chart for more accurate information.*

## Allusion, delusion, illusion

**Allusion** is a reference to something.
*Emma makes constant* ***allusions*** *to her favorite books and authors.*

**Delusion** is a mistaken belief or opinion.
*He has a* ***delusion*** *that man never set foot on the moon in 1969.*

**Illusion** is a deceptive appearance.
*This optical* ***illusion*** *is actually an effect of perspective.*

## Almost, most

**Almost** means nearly.
*Kerry touches base with work* ***almost*** *every day of his vacation.*

**Most** means the greater number of something.
*It looks like* ***most*** *of the people in the office are on vacation.*

## Aloud, out loud

**Aloud** is standard English. **Out loud** is considered colloquial.
*The teacher always enjoys reading* ***aloud*** *a few stories to the class.*

## Altar, alter

**Altar** refers to the platform at the front of a church or a temple.
*We've noticed they keep the daily prayer book on the church's* ***altar****.*

**Alter** means to change.
*The judge may* ***alter*** *her decision on TV cameras in the courtroom.*

## Alteration, altercation, alternation

**Alteration** is changing something.
*Some scientists believe gene* ***alteration*** *may raise the risk of cancer.*

**Altercation** is an argument, dispute, or fight.
*Play is stopped because of an* ***altercation*** *in the outfield stands.*

**Alternation** is constant change from one thing to another and back again.
*The doctors experimented with the close* ***alternation*** *of two remedies.*

## Alternate, alternative

**Alternate** means every other one or to change from one to another.
*Every* ***alternate*** *Friday afternoon Joe and Eric meet for a golf match.*
*Rich usually* ***alternates*** *between his three wood and driver off the tee.*

**Alternative** means a choice between two or more possibilities.
*The other* ***alternative*** *is to leave early before the late afternoon traffic.*

## Although, whereas

**Although** refers to a concession of things.
***Although** your credit card recently expired, we will honor the reservation.*

**Whereas** refers to a contrast of things.
*Your suits are quite expensive, **whereas** your shirts are quite a bargain.*

## Alumna, alumnus

**Alumna** is a former female student (Plural is *alumnae.*).
**Alumnus** is a former male student (Plural is *alumni.*).

## Amateur, novice

**Amateur** refers to someone who does the activity just as a pastime.
*Tiger Woods was an exceptional **amateur** before turning professional.*

**Novice** refers to someone who is a beginner.
*When it comes to playing golf, he's just a **novice**.*

## Ambiguous, ambivalent, indifferent

**Ambiguous** means being unclear, undefined, or subject to interpretation.
*The candidate is so **ambiguous** that very few understood his platform.*

**Ambivalent** means having mixed feelings or being uncertain.
*Jim is **ambivalent** about returning to college for more graduate work.*

**Indifferent** means being apathetic or showing no concern.
*The legislature remains **indifferent** about building a new library.*

## Amend, emend

**Amend** means to add or substantially change a document (an *amendment*).
*It's time to **amend** our organization's charter.*

**Emend** means to make changes or corrections to text (an *emendation*).
*The publisher wants to **emend** the document before the next edition.*

## Amiable, amicable

**Amiable** means agreeable, easy to deal with, or friendly.
*Rob is an **amiable** person with whom I enjoy playing a round of golf.*

**Amicable** means good willed or friendly.
*The U.S. maintains an **amicable** relationship with that country.*

## Among, amongst

**Among** is preferred in American English.

## Among, between

**Among** is used for relationships involving more than two.
*The four of them agree **among** themselves that the approach is weak.*

**Between** is usually used for relationships involving only two.
*Joseph's college choice is **between** Colorado and California.*

Note: Sometimes **between** is appropriate for more than two.
*The choice for best golfer of the 60s is **between** Arnold, Gary, and Jack.*
*We are attempting to resolve the differences **between** the four children.*

## Amoral, immoral

**Amoral** means without morality.
*They are known to be quite **amoral**, with no sense of right or wrong.*

**Immoral** means contrary to established moral standards.
*Some people may find both the book and movie **immoral**.*

## Amount, number

**Amount** refers to things that cannot be counted individually.
*Furnishing a new office complex requires a great **amount** of planning.*

**Number** refers to countable things.
*The new tenants bought a large **number** of PCs for the office complex.*

## Ample, enough

**Ample** means more than adequate in capacity, scope, or size.
*Today you have **ample** opportunity to talk with prospective clients.*

**Enough** means adequate or sufficient to satisfy a need.
*Make sure you have more than **enough** RAM to run the program.*

## Amuse, bemuse

**Amuse** means to cause to entertain, laugh, or smile.
*Jim's jokes still **amuse** us, even though we've heard them all before.*

**Bemuse** means to bewilder, confuse, or stupefy.
*The change in game tactics appears to **bemuse** our opponents.*

## Anecdote, antidote

**Anecdote** is a short account (usually funny) about a particular incident.
*Alex told us many amusing **anecdotes** about his time in college.*

**Antidote** is a medicine or remedy for fighting poison or disease.
*The doctor always prescribes **antidotes** to counteract any poison.*

## Annihilate, decimate

**Annihilate** means to destroy something completely.
*The chemical company used a spray to **annihilate** the weeds in the yard.*

**Decimate** means to destroy a large part of something.
*The strong weed killer could **decimate** many parts of the lawn.*

## Annual APR

Redundancy. **APR** means *Annual Percentage Rate*. Just use **APR**.

## Annunciate, enunciate

**Annunciate**, a rare word, means to announce or proclaim something.
*In the event of trouble, the system **annunciates** an audible alarm.*

**Enunciate** means to pronounce, articulate, or set forth precisely.
*He spurts words almost faster than he can **enunciate** them properly.*
*These statements **enunciate** their position on human rights issues.*

## Antagonist, protagonist

**Antagonist** refers to an adversary or opponent.
*Once close friends, they became **antagonists** in business later in life.*

**Protagonist** refers to a leading character in a play, novel, or story.
*The **protagonist** in tonight's play also serves as the narrator.*

**Protagonist**, meaning a proponent, is becoming more common.
*Tony has long been a **protagonist** of solar energy and reduced emissions.*

## Ante, anti

**Ante** means before or in front of something.
*The abbreviation A.M. stands for **ante** meridian, meaning before noon.*

**Anti** means against or opposed to something.
*The doctor needs an **antitoxin** to combat the poison.*

## Antecedence, antecedents

**Antecedence** is the act of going before in time.
*The reservation should be made with at least 1 month of **antecedence**.*

**Antecedents** are people or things that have gone before.
*Peg's **antecedents** left her a fortune, and she wisely invested all of it.*

## Anticipate, expect

**Anticipate** means to foresee and prepare for something.
*The college **anticipates** a large enrollment jump for next year.*

**Expect** means to look forward to the likely occurrence of something.
*The college **expects** more than half of the senior class to get job offers.*

## Anxious, eager

**Anxious** means nervous, worried, or filled with anxiety.
*Harry is **anxious** about his final grades in math and science.*

**Eager** means looking forward to or earnestly longing.
*Greg is **eager** to see how well he did in math and science.*

## Any body, anybody

**Any body** refers to any single person or thing.
*Did you talk with **any body** in the administration about the problem?*

**Anybody** refers to any person.
***Anybody** can talk to the administration about the problem.*

## Any more, anymore

**Any more** means no more.

*Annie and Mary do not want* ***any more*** *problems with their cars.*

**Anymore** means now.
*Our friends do not live here* ***anymore****, and we certainly miss them.*

## Any one, anyone

**Any one** refers to any single person or thing.
*Did you listen to* ***any one*** *of the new Christmas CDs?*

**Anyone** refers to any person.
*Did* ***anyone*** *in the class see the solar eclipse yesterday?*

## Any way, anyway

**Any way** means by a choice of methods.
*Josh tries to improve his car's performance* ***any way*** *he possibly can.*

Anyway means in any case or nevertheless.
***Anyway****, George is still attending the concert despite his late start.*

## Anyways, anywheres

Always use **anyway** and **anywhere**.

## Apportion, portion, proportion

**Apportion** means to distribute or divide in some way.
*The attorney wants to* ***apportion*** *the estate's shares of stock evenly.*

**Portion**, the noun, means a limited amount of something.
*The family wants to leave a big* ***portion*** *of the estate to charity.*

**Portion,** the verb, is a synonym for *apportion* (distribute or divide).
*The family wants to* ***portion*** *part of the estate to charity.*

**Proportion** means a ratio of one thing to another.
*The* ***proportion*** *of golfers to tennis players increases every year.*

## Appose, oppose

**Appose** means to place near one another or juxtapose.
*The box's edges should be accurately* ***apposed*** *and slightly turned in.*

**Oppose** means to act adversely or in opposition.
*The Senator says she would definitely* ***oppose*** *the bill if put to a vote.*

## Apposite, opposite

**Apposite** means appropriate, pertinent, or suitable.
*Her style of acting and singing is* ***apposite*** *for the lead part in the play.*

**Opposite** means altogether different or to the contrary.
*The producer has an* ***opposite*** *view about casting for the lead part.*

## Appraise, apprise

**Appraise** means to estimate, evaluate, or judge something.
*Have someone* ***appraise*** *your ring so you can properly insure it.*

**Apprise** means to advise or inform people of a situation.
*Please* ***apprise*** *the accused person of his constitutional rights.*

## Apt, likely

**Apt** refers to a habitual tendency.
*Religious people are **apt** to pray and attend services regularly.*

**Likely** refers to a high probability.
*It's **likely** we will see many of our grandchildren during the holidays.*

## Arc, ark

**Arc** refers to something shaped with a curved or bowed line.
*In geometry, a segment of a curve is called an **arc**.*

**Ark** refers to a large, flat-bottomed boat.
*In the Old Testament, Noah built an **ark** for survival.*

## Arctic, artic

Always use **arctic**, not **artic**, as in **Arctic** Circle.

## Area, aria

**Area** refers to a region or section.
*What **area** of hardware engineering is your specialty?*

**Aria** refers to a solo vocal piece.
*When the lead tenor finished his **aria**, the crowd graciously applauded.*

## Arraignment, indictment

**Arraignment** refers to formally calling a defendant to answer a charge.
*The judge postponed the **arraignment** and bail hearing for a week.*

**Indictment** refers to formally charging a defendant with a crime.
*The grand jury handed up an **indictment** against five people.*

## Arrant, errant

**Arrant** means confirmed, downright, or extreme.
*We found the entire story nothing short of **arrant** nonsense.*

**Errant** means wandering or roving.
*Ray's **errant** tee shot on the last hole cost him the tournament.*

## Artisan, artist, artiste

**Artisan** refers to anyone manually skilled in a product or trade.
*Rich is an accomplished **artisan** whose passion is watercolor painting.*

**Artist** refers to anyone engaged in the fine or performing arts.
*Marcel Marceau was a popular pantomime **artist**.*

**Artiste** refers to an entertainer or anyone skilled in a special craft.
*The chef at Lake Mohonk is considered a real **artiste**.*

## As, like

**As** is a conjunction and should be followed by a subject and verb.
*In the winter, he hibernates **as** a bear does.*

**Like** is a preposition and should be followed by an object.
*In the winter, he hibernates **like** a bear.*

## As if, as though

Either phrase is acceptable, but strict grammarians prefer **as though.**
*You describe the film's details **as though** you have seen it many times.*

## As time passed, as time progressed

Use **as time passed** because time does not *progress.*
***As time passed,** the animal became more domesticated.*

## Ascent, assent

**Ascent** means an upward climb or any movement upward.
*The mountain's slight **ascent** requires little climbing experience.*

**Assent** means to agree or concur with something.
*The teacher **assented** to accepting a late paper.*

## Assay, essay

**Assay,** a verb, means to evaluate, examine, or analyze.
*Take time to **assay** the information before drawing a conclusion.*

**Essay,** a verb, means to make an attempt.
*The baby boy **essayed** a few wobbly steps last week.*

**Essay,** a noun, is a short composition expressing the author's opinion.
*Diane has to write a five-page **essay** on Tolstoy for her literature class.*

## Assert, claim

**Assert** means to state or express firmly and positively.
*The party's leader* ***asserts*** *she could never support such a bill.*

**Claim** means to demand or ask for as one's own.
*Because it is his birthday, Larry is* ***claiming*** *the first piece of cake.*

## Assume, presume

**Assume** means to take for granted without evidence.
*Do not* ***assume*** *fluoride is in your drinking water.*

**Presume** means to take for granted, usually because evidence exists.
*Because the van is being serviced, we* ***presume*** *it is not running well.*

## Assure, ensure, insure

**Assure** means to make confident or promise.
*I* ***assure*** *you the package is in today's mail.*

**Ensure** means to make certain something will happen.
*Mailing the package by Friday* ***ensures*** *a Monday delivery.*

**Insure** means to buy insurance.
*Because of its value, we made sure to* ***insure*** *the package.*

## ATM machine

Redundancy. **ATM** means *Automated Teller Machine*. Just use **ATM**.

## Attain, obtain

**Attain** means to accomplish something.
*We wish Scott well in striving to **attain** his educational goals.*

**Obtain** means to get possession of something.
*Scott is determined to **obtain** his doctorate degree by next year.*

## Auger, augur

**Auger** refers to a tool for drilling holes.
*Andy uses a gas-powered **auger** to drill holes for deck supports.*

**Augur** means to predict or to be a sign of something.
*Recent developments could **augur** change for the car industry.*

## Augment, supplement

**Augment** means to increase or magnify in size, degree, or effect.
*Some people **augment** their income with businesses on the Internet.*

**Supplement** means to add something or make up for a deficiency.
*The doctor suggests that Laura **supplement** her diet with vitamins.*

## Aural, oral

**Aural** refers to the ear or to the sense of hearing.
*The young class has more success learning by **aural** methods.*

**Oral** refers to things of the mouth.
*The hygienist always does an **oral** exam before the cleaning.*

## Authoritarian, authoritative

**Authoritarian** means requiring absolute obedience to authority.
*Does **authoritarian** government always involve censorship?*

**Authoritative** means arising from or approved from proper authority.
*He is publishing an **authoritative** guide on eating and sleeping right.*

## Avenge, revenge

**Avenge** means to seek a fair settlement for a wrong.
*The basketball team hopes to **avenge** last year's tough loss to Newburgh.*

**Revenge** means to retaliate for a wrong.
***Revenge** is a major theme in Shakespeare's "The Tragedy of Hamlet".*

## Avert, avoid, divert

**Avert** means to prevent or ward off something.
*Moderate exercise and diet can help **avert** the middle-age weight gain.*

**Avoid** means to shun or stay clear of something.
*Tom tries to **avoid** the tough questions at a press conference.*

**Divert** means to turn aside, distract, or turn from one course to another.
*That feature allows you to **divert** an incoming call to any cellular phone.*

## Avocation, vocation

**Avocation** refers to a hobby or something one does outside of regular work.
*Celeste's true **avocation** is gardening around her house.*

**Vocation** refers to a profession, principal endeavor, or source of livelihood.
*As with any* ***vocation****, you need to learn about what you are embracing.*

## Avow, vouch

**Avow** means to admit or declare it publicly.
*I can* ***avow*** *that the quality of education at Potsdam State is excellent.*

**Vouch** means to produce evidence in support of something or someone.
*I can* ***vouch*** *for your dedication, honesty, and sincerity in this matter.*

## Awhile, a while

**Awhile** is an adverb that means for a time.
*Tom and Linda are deciding whether to stay* ***awhile*** *in Otego.*

**A while** is a noun phrase used as the object of the prepositions *for* and *in.*
*Tom and Linda have decided to stay for* ***a while*** *in Otego.*
*In* ***a while****, Tom and Linda leave Otego for good.*

# B

*"The ill and unfitting choice of words wonderfully obstructs the understanding."* — Francis Bacon

## Backward, backwards

**Backward** is preferred in American usage.

## Bad, badly

**Bad** is an adjective describing nouns or pronouns.
*Our family has a **bad** feeling about the whole thing.*
*John felt **bad** about missing Karen's surprise party.*

**Badly** is an adverb describing verbs.
*Despite few rehearsals, the band is not playing **badly**.*

## Baited, bated

**Baited** means to entice or lure something.
*We **baited** the mousetrap with peanut butter and not cheese.*

**Bated** means to lessen the force or intensity of something.
*Celie and Bill waited with **bated** breath to see who won the tournament.*

## Baleful, baneful

**Baleful** refers to something that menaces or foreshadows evil.
*The teacher's **baleful** look helped silence the noisy students.*

**Baneful** refers to something harmful or destructive.
*The aggressive virus is having **baneful** effects on the farmer's cattle.*

## Baloney, bologna

**Baloney** refers to nonsense, and **bologna** refers to sausage or lunch meat.

## Batter, dough

**Batter** is a thin mixture of flour and liquid (usually poured).
*Brian is whipping up some **batter** for more blueberry pancakes.*

**Dough** is a thick mixture of flour, liquid, and other things (usually rolled).
*Last year Steve sold frozen cookie **dough** to raise money for his class.*

## Bazaar, bizarre

**Bazaar** refers to a market where miscellaneous goods are sold.
*Nancy and Joanie usually travel to a local **bazaar** to look for antiques.*

**Bizarre** means strange, weird, or out of the ordinary.
*His **bizarre** behavior disrupts an entire class.*

## Be sure and, be sure to

**Be sure to** is the correct phrase.
*Please **be sure to** leave an e-mail address and telephone number.*

## Because of, due to

**Because of** refers to cause and effect.
***Because of** the band canceling, ticket holders are quite upset.*

**Due to** should be used with a linking verb (*is*, *are*, *was*, *were*, etc.).
*The band's cancellation is **due to** poor ticket sales.*

## Behest, request

**Behest**, a formal word, refers to an authoritative command or urging.
*At his **bequest**, we made an appointment to see the dentist immediately.*

**Request** refers to asking for something.
*The dentist **requests** that we try to avoid any hard candy.*

## Being as, being that

Avoid these phrases in writing. Use ***because*** instead.
***Because** my car broke down, I missed my starting time.*

## Bemuse, amuse

*See entry for **Amuse, bemuse**.*

## Benefactor, beneficiary

**Benefactor** refers to someone who provides a gift.
*The university recognizes that Jim is a long-time **benefactor**.*

**Beneficiary** refers to someone who receives something.
*Tim was the* ***beneficiary*** *of many leadership awards in high school.*

## Beside, besides

**Beside** as a preposition means next to or compared with something.
*The commissioner sat* ***beside*** *him at the awards dinner.*
***Beside*** *other homework, I have a meeting tonight.*

**Besides** as a preposition means in addition to something.
***Besides*** *the Titleist driver, Andrew uses the new Nike golf ball.*

**Besides** as an adverb means moreover.
***Besides,*** *Al needs more than expensive golf clubs to lower his score.*

**Besides** as an adjective means otherwise.
*Who* ***besides*** *me likes his latest book?*

## Between, among

*See entry for* ***Among, between.***

## Between you and I, between you and me

Always use **between you and me.**

All prepositions, such as *between*, take pronouns in the **objective** case (*it, her, him, me, them, us, you*) not in the nominative case (*he, I, it, she, they, we, you*) or possessive case (*her, hers, his, its, mine, my, our, ours, their, theirs, your, yours*).

*Just* ***between you and me,*** *we are having a party for the Rogers family.*

## Biannual, biennial

**Biannual**, a synonym for *semiannual*, means twice a year.
*Donna and John make **biannual** visits to North Carolina each year.*

**Biennial** means once every 2 years.
*The car registration is due for its **biennial** renewal.*

## Bilateral, multilateral, unilateral

**Bilateral**, meaning two-sided, refers to two agreeing entities.
*The city has a **bilateral** agreement between the two sports teams.*

**Multilateral**, meaning many-sided, refers to more than two agreeing entities.
*The company has a **multilateral** agreement with all three investors.*

**Unilateral**, meaning one-sided, refers to an entity acting alone.
*The U.S. reached a **unilateral** agreement on free trade with that country.*

## Bimonthly, semimonthly

**Bimonthly** means occurring every 2 months.
*We bought the refreshments for the **bimonthly** status meeting.*

**Semimonthly** means occurring twice a month.
*Our **semimonthly** status reports are due the 15th and 30th of each month.*

Note: The same rules apply to *biweekly*, *biyearly*, *semiweekly*, and *semiyearly*.

## Bisect, dissect

**Bisect** means to cut in two equal or identical parts.
*The diagonals of a parallelogram **bisect** each other.*

**Dissect** means to cut apart and examine something.
*The movie critics plan to **dissect** the director's next film.*

## Blackout, brownout

Concerning power failures:

**Blackout** is a total electrical power failure over a large area.
***Blackouts** affected sections of the U.S. and Canada in 1965 and 1989.*

**Brownout** is a brief interruption or temporary drop of electrical power.
*A **brownout** caused my computer screen to flicker a few times.*

## Blatant, flagrant

**Blatant** means calling attention to something.
*We made a **blatant** mistake by overlooking Gary's contributions.*

**Flagrant** means notoriously evil, bad, or objectionable.
*The crew of the ship had an open and **flagrant** mutiny.*

## Bloc, block

**Bloc** is a coalition of people, groups, or nations with the same goal.
*The U.S. and England formed a new **bloc** of countries promoting trade.*

Use **block** for all other meanings.

## Blond, blonde

**Blond** refers to a boy or a man. **Blonde** refers to a girl or a woman.

## Boar, boor, bore

**Boar** refers to a male pig.
*The wild **boar** was first bred as a domestic animal many years ago.*

**Boor** refers to a crude, unrefined, or insensitive person.
*He sometimes can be a loud, obnoxious **boor** during our meetings.*

**Bore** refers to being dull, tiresome, or tedious.
*Reading was a **bore** until he discovered Harry Potter books.*

## Born, borne

**Born** means having been given birth to a person or animal.
*Bruce was **born** on this earth to run.*

**Borne** means to be carried by something or to endure something.
*Lyme disease is the most common form of tick-**borne** disease in the U.S.*
*We have **borne** their mistakes with the patience of a saint.*

## Bouillon, bullion

**Bouillon** refers to a clear, seasoned soup usually made from lean beef.
*Their **bouillon** has no MSG and is less than 0.5 grams of fat per serving.*

**Bullion** refers to gold or silver.
*In London, brokers of **bullion** act as agents for buyers and sellers.*

## Boycott, embargo

**Boycott** is the refraining of business or social relations to express protest.
*The consumers are promoting a* ***boycott*** *of all the company's products.*

**Embargo** is a prohibition by a government on trade with a foreign nation.
*In 1987, we imposed a trade* ***embargo*** *on imports to the U.S. from Iran.*

## Braise, braze

**Braise** means to cook slowly under a covered container.
*Helen* ***braises*** *all her meats and vegetables in lemon juice and butter.*

**Braze** means to solder something.
*The plumber needs to* ***braze*** *all the pipe fittings in the house.*

## Breach, breech

**Breach** is an infraction or violation of some kind.
*By not being on the movie set, Frank is guilty of a* ***breach*** *of contract.*

Use **breech** for all other meanings, such as ***breech*** *delivery.*

## Breadth, breath, breathe

**Breadth** refers to distance, width, or scope.
*Damian's success reflects the depth and* ***breadth*** *of his experience.*

**Breath** is the noun and **breathe** is the verb.
*We typically take several* ***breaths*** *when we* ***breathe*** *heavily.*

## Bridal, bridle

**Bridal** refers to a marriage ceremony.
*The* ***bridal*** *party stayed until the late hours.*

**Bridle** refers to the harness on a horse's head or to horseback riding.
*Make sure the horse's* ***bridle*** *is not too tight but yet snug.*
*Though the* ***bridle*** *path is long and winding, it is still enjoyable.*

**Bridle** also refers to restraint or control.
*The players should* ***bridle*** *their appetites before exercising.*

## Bring, take

**Bring** means moving toward someone or something.
*When you are finished writing the proposal, please* ***bring*** *it to my office.*

**Take** means moving away from someone or something.
*When I am finished reviewing the proposal, please* ***take*** *it to your office.*

## British Isles, Great Britain, United Kingdom

The **British Isles** consists of the **United Kingdom** and its islands (Orkneys, Shetlands, and the Isle of Man). **Great Britain** consists of England, Scotland, and Wales. The **United Kingdom** consists of Great Britain and Northern Ireland.

## Broach, brooch

**Broach** means to open, introduce, or bring up something.
*Do not **broach** that sensitive subject with the other team members.*

**Brooch** refers to a pin or ornament with a clasp.
*Donna wore an expensive **brooch** to her high school reunion.*

## Broken, busted

Prefer **broken. Busted** is considered a nonstandard word. Avoid its use.
*Scott suffered a **broken** leg during Monday's football practice.*

## Brother-in-laws, brothers-in-law

**Brothers-in-law** is the correct phrase.

## Build off of, build on

**Build on** is the correct phrase.
***Build on** the successes you and your team have attained this year.*

## Burglary, robbery, theft

**Burglary** is the breaking into a building to steal something.
*House **burglaries** can result from thieves entering via unlocked doors.*

**Robbery** is the taking of one's property by possible threat or force.
*Twenty people were involved in London's Great Train **Robbery** of 1963.*

**Theft** is the taking of one's property without threat or force.
*Identity* ***theft*** *is a fast growing crime in America.*

(Note: *Larceny* is the legal term for theft or stealing.)

# C

*"An unusual word should be shunned as a ship would shun a reef."*
— Julius Caesar

## Cache, cash

**Cache** is a hiding place.
*The bears found a **cache** of food belonging to some hunters.*

**Cache** is also small, fast memory that holds recently accessed data.
*Could the **cache** handle the extra memory requirements?*

**Cash** refers to ready money.
*Please attach a copy of your **cash** receipt to the rebate form.*

## CAD design

Redundancy. CAD means *Computer-Assisted Design*. Just use **CAD**.

## Calendar, calender

**Calendar** is the correct spelling for a system of recording time.
**Calender** is an old word that refers to a machine used in finishing paper and cloth.

## Callous, callus

**Callous** refers to having an unfeeling attitude.
*Perhaps you're being too **callous** about their unfortunate situation.*

**Callus** refers to a thickening or hardening of the skin.
*The tight running shoes gave Austin a **callus** on his foot.*

## Calvary, cavalry

**Calvary**, with a capital *C*, is the place in Jerusalem where Christ died.
**Cavalry** are soldiers mounted on horseback.

## Can, may

**Can** refers to capability.
*The server **can** support up to 500 users.*

**May** refers to permission or possibility.
*You **may** start working on the project now.*
*The students **may** finish the school year early.*

## Can not, cannot

**Cannot** is always one word.

## Cancel, delay, postpone

**Cancel** means to stop something with no intent to reschedule.
*After 3 years, Chris and Eric decided to **cancel** their subscription.*

**Delay** means to put off until further notice.
*The heavy rains could **delay** the game for several hours.*

**Postpone** means to stop something but with the intent to reschedule.
*I hope the committee does not **postpone** the test another week.*

## Canter, cantor

**Canter** refers to a horse's gait.
*The thoroughbred's* ***canter*** *is one of strength, agility, and grace.*

**Cantor** refers to a singer.
*Lori is the* ***cantor*** *for this Sunday's service.*

## Canvas, canvass

**Canvas** is the cloth used in making tents or sails, or what painters use.
*You can enlarge photographs on* ***canvas*** *to look like a textured painting.*

**Canvass** is soliciting political support from voters before an election.
*Rob opted not to* ***canvass*** *in this year's Democratic primary.*

## Capacity, ability

*See entry for* ***Ability, capacity.***

## Capital, capitol

**Capital** refers to money, equipment, property, uppercase letters, form of punishment, architecture, or the location of a government seat.

Examples:
The **capital** gain tax, **capital** letters, **capital** punishment, the pillar's **cap-ital,** or the **capital** of New York State is Albany.

**Capitol** refers to buildings in which state or national government meet. (The *C* in **Capitol** is always uppercase.)

Examples:
The **Capitol** in downtown Albany, the U.S. **Capitol** in D.C., or **Capitol** Hill.

## Capitulate, recapitulate

**Capitulate** means to surrender, come to terms, or acquiesce.
*NATO is unable to force the country to **capitulate** to its demands.*

**Recapitulate** means to sum up, review briefly, or repeat in concise form.
*Let us **recapitulate** what we have learned so far today.*

## Carat, caret, carrot, karat

**Carat** is a measurement (200 milligrams) used in weighing gemstones.
*Ty gave Jenna an engagement ring that has a 1.5 **carat** diamond setting.*

**Caret** is a proofreader's mark to indicate insertion. It's also used in math to indicate exponentiation.
*Editors are known for inserting many **carets** on a writer's first draft.*
*If the **caret** is not in the formula, you'll get an entirely different answer.*

**Carrot** is the orange root vegetable that Bugs Bunny enjoys eating.
*Although **carrots** can endure heat, they grow best when planted in spring.*

**Karat** is a measurement showing the quantity of pure gold to an alloy in a gemstone. The measurement uses a base of 24 units. Pure gold, which is 24/24ths gold, is technically called 24-karat gold.
*All their 12-**karat** jewelry is on sale through next weekend.*

## Cardinal numbers, ordinal numbers

**Cardinal numbers** (*1, 2, 3,* and so on) refer to quantity but not order.
*We arrived 2 hours early for the concert.*

**Ordinal numbers** (*first, second, third,* and so on) refer to position or numerical sequence.
*Our seats are in the* ***third*** *row of the theater.*

## Careen, career, carom

**Careen** means to swerve or tilt while in motion.
*Despite suspension improvements, the car* ***careened*** *during the test.*

**Career** means to move at full speed.
*We held our breath as the racing car* ***careered*** *down the track.*

**Carom** means to collide and rebound.
*We held our breath as the racing car* ***caromed*** *off the wall.*

## Carnivorous, herbivorous, omnivorous

**Carnivorous** refers to eating meat (or flesh).
*The biggest* ***carnivorous*** *dinosaurs were from the Cretaceous period.*

**Herbivorous** refers to eating only plants (vegetarian).
*Iguanas and tortoises are typical* ***herbivorous*** *reptiles.*

**Omnivorous** refers to eating everything.
*An* ***omnivorous*** *diet consists of meats, fruits, grains, and vegetables.*

## CBT training

Redundancy. **CBT** means *Computer Based Training*. Just use **CBT**.

## CD-ROM disc

Redundancy. **CD-ROM** means *Compact Disc-Read Only Memory*. Just use **CD-ROM**.

## Cement, concrete

**Cement** is a powdery binding material that consists of clay and limestone. **Concrete** is a mixture of sand, gravel, and other materials all held together by the **cement**.
*The workers are installing a new* ***concrete*** (not ***cement***) *sidewalk.*

## Censor, censure

**Censor**, as a verb, means to remove or suppress objectionable material.
*Some people feel that Congress has the right to* ***censor*** *the Internet.*

**Censor**, as a noun, is the person examining certain material.
*Are the TV* ***censors*** *approving that controversial subject?*

**Censure** means to blame, criticize strongly, or condemn something.
*The principal* ***censured*** *a few students for the graffiti on the walls.*

## Center around

This is a physical impossibility. Use *center about*, *center in*, or *center on*.
*Next week's Open House* ***centers on*** *the theme of Quality at Work.*

## Ceremonial, ceremonious

**Ceremonial** means being proper for a ceremony.
*Sandy wore her traditional* ***ceremonial*** *dress to the awards banquet.*

**Ceremonious** means being done in great ceremony (politely or formally).
*The King offered a* ***ceremonious*** *toast to everyone at the gala.*

## Cession, session

**Cession** refers to an act of ceding (surrendering) to another.
*It took the committee over 2 years to ratify the* ***cession*** *agreement.*

**Session** refers to a meeting or term.
*Scott is taking just one course during the school's summer* ***session.***

## Chafe, chaff

**Chafe** means to irritate or annoy something.
*These new running shoes* ***chafe*** *my feet.*

**Chaff**, a verb, means to tease good-naturedly.
*Patty's new teammates* ***chaffed*** *her for being late again.*

**Chaff**, a noun, are husks separated from seeds during threshing.
*Karen and Brian literally separated the wheat from the* ***chaff.***

## Chantey, shanty

**Chantey** refers to a song sung by sailors while working.
*As the ship's crew washed the deck, the captain requested a* ***chantey.***

**Shanty** refers to a roughly built shack.
*While stranded on the island, the crew lived in a small* ***shanty.***

## Character, reputation

**Character** refers to the actual personality of a person.
*His spontaneous reaction is completely out of* ***character*** *for him.*

**Reputation** refers to the external perception of a person.
*In spite of her* ***reputation*** *as fair, many are stunned with the decision.*

## Childish, childlike

**Childish** means inappropriately acting like or resembling a child.
*The painting looks like* ***childish*** *scribble rather than art.*

**Childlike** means to retain some of the positive attributes of childhood.
*Even in his 60s, Ken retains a* ***childlike*** *enthusiasm for popular music.*

## Chord, cord

**Chord** refers to musical notes.
*The clever song consists of just three* ***chords.***

**Cord** refers to a vocal cord, a cord of wood, or a rope.
*The constant high notes strained his vocal* ***cords.***
*We bought four* ***cords*** *of wood for next winter.*
*Please pull the* ***cord*** *when you get to the front door.*

## Chronic, acute

*See entry for* ***Acute, chronic.***

## Cite, sight, site

**Cite** means to quote or mention something.
*When you write a technical paper for Dr. Hards,* ***cite*** *your references.*

**Sight** is something seen, an ability to see, the foreseeable future, or an optical instrument.
*The passengers on the ship soon caught* ***sight*** *of the island.*
*The passengers* ***sighted*** *the island from a great distance.*
*The people saw no compromise or solution in* ***sight****.*
*John is adjusting the* ***sight*** *on his rifle.*

**Site** refers to a location.
*This looks like a good* ***site*** *to build a new house.*

## Claim, assert

*See entry for* ***Assert, claim.***

## Cliché, clique

**Cliché** refers to overused expressions.
*Good writers try to avoid using* ***clichés*** *in their writing.*

**Clique** refers to a small, exclusive group of people.
*Many* ***cliques*** *exist in their large high school.*

## Click, press, type

**Click** means pressing and releasing the mouse button once.
***Click*** *the icon on the desktop.*

**Press** means to put force on something.
***Press** the Reset button on the furnace just once.*

**Type** means pressing a character key on a keyboard.
***Type** the letter A.*

## Climactic, climatic

**Climactic** refers to the culmination of events (a climax).
*The special effects in the **climactic** scene of the film are impressive.*

**Climatic** refers to meteorological conditions (the weather).
*The third round finished just before severe **climatic** conditions arrived.*

## Climax, acme

*See entry for **Acme, climax.***

## CNN network

Redundancy. CNN means *Cable News Network*. Just use CNN.

## Cohere, adhere

*See entry for **Adhere, cohere.***

## Collaborate, corroborate

**Collaborate** means to aid, cooperate, or work together.
*The church and I **collaborated** on the Christmas project for the needy.*

**Corroborate** means to strengthen by confirming something.
*The witness **corroborated** the defendant's testimony during the trial.*

## Collectable, collectible

Either spelling is acceptable.

## Collision, collusion

**Collision** refers to a crash.
*The **collision** of the two ships raises many questions.*

**Collusion** refers to a secret agreement between parties.
*The high prices this summer could be a **collusion** among the companies.*

## Cologne, perfume

**Cologne** is a weak, inexpensive fragrance; **perfume** is a strong, expensive fragrance.

## Common, mutual, ordinary, popular

**Common** means widespread or prevalent.
*Mosquitoes are **common** disease carriers.*

**Mutual** means shared by two or more parties.
***Mutual** trust is a necessary ingredient for a long-term relationship.*

**Ordinary** means plain or undistinguished.
*We sometimes take the **ordinary** things of life for granted.*

**Popular** means especially liked, preferred, or appreciated.
*Jerry Lewis films are quite **popular** in Europe, especially France.*

## Compare and contrast

Redundancy. When you **compare** things, you note both differences and similarities. When you contrast things, you note just the differences. Therefore, use **compare** or **contrast** separately but not together.

## Compared to, compared with

**Compared to** means to examine similarities or to liken one thing to another.
***Compared to** our city, your city has about the same number of people.*
*The famous author and entertainer **compared** his world **to** a stage.*

**Compared with** means to examine dissimilarities.
*As **compared with** 1996, the election of 2000 was undecided for weeks.*

## Complacent, complaisant

**Complacent** refers to a feeling of self-satisfaction.
*After having a string of successes, the film director grew **complacent**.*

**Complaisant** refers to a willingness to comply or oblige.
*An energetic and **complaisant** guide took us on a tour of West Point.*

## Complement, compliment

**Complement**, as a noun, means the sense of completion.
*A **complement** of four people would bring the staff to nine.*

**Complement**, as a verb, means to be complementary to something.
*The four new people would* ***complement*** *the rest of the staff.*

**Compliment**, as a noun, means an expression or act of courtesy or praise.
*The supervisor gave the staff a* ***compliment*** *on its efficient job.*

**Compliment**, as a verb, means to admire, praise, or respect something.
*The supervisor regularly* ***compliments*** *the staff on its efficient work.*

## Compose, comprise

**Compose** means to create or to make up the whole.
*John Williams* ***composes*** *musical scores for many Spielberg films.*
*Five thousand songs* ***compose*** *the college's music library.*

**Comprise** means to consist of something.
*The college's music library* ***comprises*** *5,000 songs.*

Memory hook: The whole **comprises** the parts, and the parts **compose** the whole.

## Comprehensible, comprehensive

**Comprehensible** means understandable or intelligible.
*Despite all the technical jargon, the book is quite* ***comprehensible.***

**Comprehensive** means comprising many things or large in scope.
*Jim did a* ***comprehensive*** *study on the Internet's impact to the economy.*

## Compulsion, compunction

**Compulsion** refers to a forced impulse, compliance, or drive.
*John Lennon had a **compulsion** to make the Beatles a top rock band.*

**Compunction** refers to remorse or regret for one's actions.
*Dave showed much **compunction** at the thought of leaving his old job.*

## Compulsive, compulsory, impulsive

**Compulsive** refers to being obsessive about something.
*Tom is a **compulsive** Giants fan during the football season.*

**Compulsory** refers to being obligated to do something.
*Les took a **compulsory** physical examination for his new job.*

**Impulsive** refers to doing things on the spur of the moment.
*Occasionally Ed gets **impulsive** and buys an expensive car.*

## Concert, recital

**Concert** refers to a performance given by two or more people.
*The Beatles gave their last American **concert** in San Francisco in 1966.*

**Recital** refers to a performance given by one person (a soloist).
*Her Christmas piano **recital** went better than we expected.*

## Concurrent, consecutive

**Concurrent** means simultaneous or happening at the same time.
*Management is holding **concurrent** meetings to announce the changes.*

**Consecutive** means successive or following one after the other.
*The pitcher threw six **consecutive** strikes in the last inning.*

## Conducive to, conducive with

**Conducive to**, meaning to bring about, is the preferred phrase.
*Good working conditions can be **conducive to** more productivity.*

## Confidant, confident

**Confidant** refers to a trustworthy friend.
*Linda is her **confidant** as well as a technical advisor on many issues.*

**Confident** refers to being self assured.
*Liam is very **confident** that his unique house design will sell.*

## Congenial, congenital, genial

**Congenial** means having the same nature, disposition, or tastes.
*We continue to work in a **congenial** atmosphere that all of us enjoy.*

**Congenital** means existing in an individual since birth.
*His disease can be traced to a **congenital** disorder.*

**Genial** means agreeable, pleasing, or compatible.
*The retirees are experiencing a **genial** climate in Arizona.*

## Connote, denote

**Connote** means to imply or suggest something.
*We foster an environment that **connotes** innovation and teamwork.*

**Denote** means to indicate or refer to specifically.
*The symbol for pi* ***denotes*** *the number 3.14159.*

## Conscience, conscious

**Conscience** means a sense of right and wrong.
*Obviously his* ***conscience*** *did not bother him about the tough decision.*

**Conscious** means to be aware of something.
*Margie made a* ***conscious*** *decision to practice her piano lessons daily.*

## Consequent, subsequent

**Consequent** means following as a direct result.
*Jan's excellent evaluation and* ***consequent*** *pay raise made her day.*

**Subsequent** means occurring after.
***Subsequent*** *to the installation, my desktop icons would not load.*

## Consistently, constantly

**Consistently** means steadfast, unwavering, or without change.
*Airline tickets* ***consistently*** *rank among the popular items on the Internet.*

**Constantly** means unceasing, perpetual, or without interruption.
*Training is vital in a* ***constantly*** *changing technical world.*

## Consul, council, counsel

**Consul** is an official representing one's country in a foreign country.
*A new* ***consul*** *was appointed last week for the Republic of Chad.*

**Council** is a group of people appointed or elected to make decisions.
*Most cities and towns have a **council** that governs their area.*

**Counsel**, as a noun, is an attorney; as a verb, it means to give advice.
*The **counsel** (attorney) did an excellent job with our case.*
*The social worker tried to **counsel** the disgruntled family.*

## Contagious, infectious

**Contagious** refers to diseases obtained through some physical contact.
*If you deal with **contagious** diseases, wash and disinfect your hands well.*

**Infectious** refers to diseases spread through air, water, and other means.
*They are exposed to not only chemicals but **infectious** things as well.*

Note: In figurative use, these words can be synonymous.
*Her optimistic and humorous mood is **infectious*** (or ***contagious***).

## Contemptible, contemptuous

**Contemptible** means worthy of contempt, deserving scorn, or disdain.
*The members think Keith's actions on the board are **contemptible**.*

**Contemptuous** means expressing a feeling of contempt for something.
*The members risk disciplinary action for making **contemptuous** remarks.*

## Contentious, controversial

**Contentious** refers to people being argumentative or quarrelsome.
*The measure was defeated after a long, **contentious** House debate.*

**Controversial** refers to subjects being arguable, debatable, or disputable.
*The office extended the deadline on the **controversial** licensing change.*

## Conterminous, contiguous

**Conterminous** means contained within one boundary.
*The **conterminous** U.S. excludes two states: Alaska and Hawaii.*

**Contiguous** means sharing a boundary or touching.
*Alaska and Hawaii are not **contiguous** with the other 48 states.*

## Continual, continuous

**Continual** means repeatedly or with interruptions.
*Network television **continually** interrupts movies with commercials.*

**Continuous** means constantly or without interruptions.
*Cable television **continuously** broadcasts movies without commercials.*

## Continuance, continuation

**Continuance** refers to the duration of a state or condition.
*Her **continuance** in office depends on the November election.*

**Continuation** refers to the resumption of something.
*The **continuation** of the meeting begins at 2 p.m.*

## Contrary, converse

**Contrary** means to differ or to disagree with something.
***Contrary** to belief, high cholesterol is not the only cause of heart disease.*

**Converse** means the opposite of something.
*I held the **converse** view that Barry Bonds' home run record would fall.*

## Convert into, convert to

**Convert into** means to transform or change from one thing to another.
*These tools **convert** PDF documents **into** either HTML or ASCII text.*

**Convert to** means to switch allegiance, loyalty, or obligation.
*While attending college, John **converted to** another faith.*

## Convince, persuade

**Convince** means to cause someone to believe through evidence.
*We **convinced** Fred of his outstanding record as class president.*

**Persuade** means to cause someone to act through argument or reasoning.
*The class **persuaded** Diane to run for re-election in the spring.*

## Core, corps

**Core** refers to the central or essential part.
*A **core** rule of this company includes the dress code.*

**Corps** refers to a group of people acting as a body rather than individuals.
*He and a few other people we know belong to the Peace **Corps**.*

## Corespondent, correspondent

**Corespondent** is a person charged with adultery in a divorce suit.
*In court, the **corespondent** did not acknowledge an extramarital affair.*

**Correspondent** is a communicator such as a writer.
*Kathy worked as a special* ***correspondent*** *for the network last year.*

## Corrode, erode

**Corrode** means to be eaten away by a chemical reaction.
*Most metals immediately* ***corrode*** *on contact with water.*

**Erode** means to wear away by water or wind.
*The heavy spring rains* ***eroded*** *the high cliffs by their beach house.*

Note: Both of these words can also be used figuratively.
*Mistrust can* ***corrode*** *any good business partnership.*
*Confidence in their leadership* ***eroded*** *over the years.*

## Could care less, could not care less

Though it is a tired cliché, **could not care less** is the correct phrase.
*He* ***could not care less*** *about learning how to play bridge.*

## Could have, could of

**Could have** is the correct phrase.
*During last night's meeting, you* ***could have*** *heard a pin drop.*

## Covert, overt

**Covert** means concealed, covered, or hidden.
*Mike's company provides* ***covert*** *video surveillance equipment.*

**Overt** means open to view, plain, apparent, or public.
*Great Britain continues to offer the U.S. its* ***overt*** *support.*

## CPU unit

Redundancy. CPU means *Central Processing Unit.* Just use CPU.

## Credible, creditable, credulous

**Credible** means believable.
*Though it's a strange and unusual story, it seems* ***credible.***

**Creditable** means worthy of praise or credit.
*The Moody Blues gave a* ***creditable*** *performance last month in Syracuse.*

**Credulous** means gullible.
*The* ***credulous*** *fan believes tickets are still available at this late hour.*

## Crevasse, crevice

**Crevasse** is a deep opening or crack usually found in a glacier.
*Frank is standing too close to the gaping* ***crevasse*** *of the glacier.*

**Crevice** is a narrow opening or crack in a wall, floor, rock, and so on.
*Jim found fewer rock* ***crevices*** *on that side of the mountain.*

## Criteria, criterion

**Criteria** is the plural noun form, and **criterion** is the singular noun form.

*These* ***criteria*** *are important to their everyday success.*
*The most important* ***criterion*** *for us now is a sense of humor.*

Note: Phrases such as *a criteria, one criteria,* or *this criteria* should be avoided. Also, a few writing authorities accept *criterions* as the plural of **criterion.**

## CRT tube

Redundancy. **CRT** means *Cathode Ray Tube.* Just use **CRT.**

## Cue, queue

**Cue** refers to a signal to begin something.
*The actors are getting their* ***cue*** *from the orchestra.*

**Queue** refers to people or things in line.
*Is that your document in the print* ***queue****?*

## Cynical, sarcastic, skeptical

**Cynical** means contemptuously distrustful of human nature and motives.
"*Those* ***cynical*** *men who say that democracy cannot be honest and efficient.*" — FDR

**Sarcastic** means directing bitter or caustic language against someone.
*Avoid being* ***sarcastic*** *or rude when dealing with sensitive people.*

**Skeptical** means doubting, questioning, or mistrustful.
*Candy seemed* ***skeptical*** *when we told her we are seeing a psychic.*

# D

"*A word in earnest is as good as speech.*" — Charles Dickens

## Damage, damages

**Damage** refers to destruction of some kind.
*What kind of **damage** results from a fire of that size?*

**Damages** refers to compensation awarded by a court of law.
*The court awarded substantial **damages** to the families.*

## Dare say, daresay

Either spelling is acceptable.

## DAT tape

Redundancy. DAT means *Digital Audio Tape*. Just use DAT.

## Data, datum

**Data** is the plural of **datum**.
*Computer models generated these **data**.*

Note: When **data** is used as a collective noun, it takes a singular verb.
*The online numeric **data** is restricted to privileged users.*

## Daughter-in-laws, daughters-in-law

**Daughters-in-law** is the correct phrase.

## Daylight saving time, daylight savings time

**Daylight saving time** is the correct phrase.

## DC current

Redundancy. **DC** means *Direct Current.* Just use **DC.**

## Deadly, deathly

**Deadly** means likely to cause death.
*Some snake bites in the jungle can be **deadly.***

**Deathly** means like or in the manner of death.
*The theater was **deathly** quiet as the curtain opened for the first act.*

## Dearth, plethora

**Dearth** refers to a great shortage or scarcity of something.
*We have a **dearth** of competent workers to handle the new project.*

**Plethora** refers to an abundance or excess of something.
*The holiday season brings a **plethora** of "Greatest Hits" CDs.*

## Debar, disbar

**Debar** means to bar from a place or prevent from exercising a right.
*Many states **debar** people under 21 from alcohol and tobacco.*

**Disbar** means to expel from the bar or the legal profession.
*The lawyer avoided prosecution, but attempts are being made to **disbar** him.*

## Debark, disembark

Both words mean to go ashore or to unload something. Either one is acceptable.

## Decent, descent, dissent

**Decent** means proper or honest.
*The play's interpretation was done in a **decent** manner.*
*Many people consider Rick a thoughtful and **decent** individual.*

**Descent** means a downward slope or family origin.
*The airplane's sudden **descent** alarmed many passengers.*
*When one mentions the **descent** of man, we think of Charles Darwin.*

**Dissent** means disagreement.
*No rule or guideline ever met with as much **dissent**.*

## Decided, decisive, incisive

**Decided** means clear-cut, unmistakable, or without doubt.
*The large companies have a **decided** advantage over the competitors.*

**Decisive** means being conclusive or the power to settle a dispute.
*The committee's **decisive** action gave our firm a unique advantage.*

**Incisive** means acute, cutting, or sharp.
*The company lost an **incisive** mind and an outstanding engineer.*

## Decimate, annihilate

*See entry for **Annihilate, decimate.***

## Decry, descry

**Decry** means to openly condemn or ridicule.
*The faculty has a right to **decry** the cuts in the education budget.*

**Descry** means to see or catch sight of, often from a distance.
*Some nights you can **descry** the blue whales out at sea.*

## Deduce, deduct, adduce

*See entry for **Adduce, deduce, deduct.***

## Deductive, inductive

Concerning types of reasoning:

**Deductive** means to reason from the general to the specific (top-down approach).
Example: *All people need water to survive; Bob is a person; Bob needs water to survive.*

**Inductive** means to reason from the specific to the general (bottom-up approach).
Example: *Bob needs water to survive; Bob is a typical person; all people need water to survive.*

## De facto, de jure

**De facto** means as a matter of fact or existence.
*The* ***de facto*** *speed limit for Rt. 17 on a busy afternoon is 55 m.p.h.*

**De jure** means as a matter of law or right.
*The speed limit on Rt. 17 is 65 m.p.h.* ***de jure.***

## Defective, deficient

**Defective** means faulty.
*The new scanner has a* ***defective*** *circuit board.*

**Deficient** means lacking completeness or a necessary ingredient.
*Without the lead singer, the band is* ***deficient*** *in hitting the higher notes.*

## Deference, difference, diffidence

**Deference** means courteous regard or respect.
*The political party shows a kind* ***deference*** *to the nominations.*

**Difference** means a distinguishing characteristic or disparity.
*The* ***difference*** *is in the way they present themselves to the public.*

**Diffidence** means reserved, shy, or lacking self confidence.
*Overcoming their* ***diffidence*** *may lead to better job opportunities.*

## Definite, definitive

**Definite** means to be certain, precise, explicit, or clear.
*No doubt, there is a* ***definite*** *feeling of accomplishment.*

**Definitive** means final, decisive, and authoritative.
*The interested party gave us a* ***definitive*** *answer yesterday.*

## Defuse, diffuse

**Defuse** means to remove a fuse (usually from an explosive object).
*The company hired an explosives expert to* ***defuse*** *the bomb.*

**Diffuse** means to spread something out.
*The mouse's odor* ***diffused*** *throughout the house.*

## Delay, cancel, postpone

*See entry for* ***Cancel, delay, postpone.***

## Delegate, relegate

**Delegate** means to entrust, hand over, or assign others to a task.
*The officials may* ***delegate*** *authority to the appropriate people.*

**Relegate** means to send or consign to an obscure place or position.
*He was* ***relegated*** *to a backup position on the team.*

## Delusion, allusion, illusion

*See entry for* ***Allusion, delusion, illusion.***

## Demur, demure

**Demur** means to voice opposition, objection, or delay.
*Jim may **demur** at the suggestion that we start the meeting now.*

**Demure** means modest, reserved, or shy.
*Peter appears quite **demure** considering all his accomplishments.*

## Denote, connote

*See entry for **Connote, denote.***

## Denounce, renounce

**Denounce** means to criticize or condemn something openly.
*The new drug was **denounced** as ineffective and harmful.*

**Renounce** means to give up claim to something.
*The engineer willingly **renounced** all ownership to the software.*

## Depraved, deprived

**Depraved** means morally bad or corrupt.
*A **depraved** person can easily have a bad influence on other people.*

**Deprived** means lacking economic or social necessities.
*We distributed their generous contributions to many **deprived** areas.*

## Deprecate, depreciate

**Deprecate** means to disapprove or belittle something.
*Tom **deprecated** his own key role in the company's success.*

**Depreciate** means to lower the value or worth of something.
*The economic problems caused my portfolio's value to **depreciate**.*

## Desert, dessert

**Desert**, as a noun, is a hot, dry, sandy place that has little vegetation.
*The **desert** ranges of the southwest are beautiful places to visit.*

**Desert**, as a verb, means to abandon or forsake.
*Despite financial setbacks, the team refuses to **desert** the company.*

**Dessert**, the noun, is the sweet thing one eats at the end of a meal.
*We always look to Mary for great **desserts**, especially her pies.*

## Desolate, dissolute

**Desolate** means uninhabited or miserable.
*Chris and Bill decided to retire in a **desolate** part of upstate New York.*
*The children are **desolate** over the loss of their dog last year.*

**Dissolute** means lacking in moral standards.
*They regret living such a **dissolute** lifestyle in their younger years.*

## Despatch, dispatch

**Dispatch** is preferred in American usage.

## Desperate, disparate

**Desperate** means last resort or hopeless.
*We are taking **desperate** measures to avoid another workers' strike.*

**Disparate** means completely distinct or different.
*The candidates' solutions reflect* ***disparate*** *visions of government's role.*

## Despise, hate

**Despise** means to regard with contempt or to look down on someone.
*Being from Florida, they* ***despised*** *the frigid weather we get in January.*

**Hate** means to dislike intensely or loathe.
*It's too bad that fussy eaters like Dave* ***hate*** *mayonnaise on all food.*

## Detract, distract

**Detract** means to take away a part or lessen.
*Their questionable behavior* ***detracts*** *from their accomplishments.*

**Distract** means to divert, confound, or harass.
*The noise in the balcony* ***distracted*** *Cathy's attention from the play.*

## Device, devise

**Device** refers to a gadget.
*In addition to the PC, the personal copier is a useful* ***device****.*

**Devise** means to think of something.
*The President and his staff* ***devised*** *a plan to help the economy.*

## Dexterous, dextrous

Though **dexterous** is more common, either spelling is acceptable.

## Diagnosis, prognosis

**Diagnosis** is the identification or the nature of something.
*The **diagnosis** shows a tear in the knee's cartilage.*

**Prognosis** is a forecast or prediction of the probable cause.
*The doctor offered his **prognosis** that the knee surgery would help.*

## Dialog, dialogue

Though **dialogue** is more common, either spelling is acceptable.

## Differ from, differ with

**Differ from** means to differ between one person or thing and others.
*My car **differs from** Joe's because it is equipped with more options.*

**Differ with** means to differ in opinion (disagree).
*His views on religion and creation **differed with** mine.*

## Different from, different than

**Different from** is usually preferred in American usage.
*Her car is **different from** mine in many ways.*

Note: **Different than** is sometimes preferred when a subject and verb (a clause) follow the phrase.
*Her job today is much **different than** it was 5 years ago.*

## Diminish, minimize

**Diminish** means to reduce, shrink, or make less important.
*Glycolic acid can help **diminish** facial lines and wrinkles.*

**Minimize** means to reduce to the smallest amount, degree, size, or extent.
*Exercises to the stomach, hips, and thigh muscles can **minimize** back pain.*

## Diplomat, diplomate

**Diplomat** is one skilled in negotiations, good manners, or tact.
*The **diplomat** offered an effective and peaceful resolution to the conflict.*

**Diplomate** is a physician certified as a specialist by an examining board.
*Dr. Walker is a **diplomate** of the American Board of Plastic Surgery.*

## Disapprove, disprove

**Disapprove** means to withhold approval of something.
*Do you approve or **disapprove** of the way Lou is handling his new job?*

**Disprove** means to prove the falsity of something.
*If you fail to **disprove** a claim, this does not prove it is true.*

## Disassemble, dissemble

**Disassemble** means to take apart something.
*To **disassemble** the hardware, follow the easy instructions in that book.*

**Dissemble** means to disguise or conceal behind a false appearance.
*The children tend to **dissemble** their sorrow with silence.*

## Disassociate, dissociate

Either spelling is acceptable, though **dissociate** is preferred.

## Disburse, disperse

**Disburse** means to pay out or expend.
*Accounting should **disburse** the travel compensation by next week.*

**Disperse** means to scatter.
*The road crew should **disperse** the road salt later this morning.*

## Discomfit, discomfort

**Discomfit** means to frustrate, disconcert, or baffle.
*Their questionable comments may **discomfit** the other employees.*

**Discomfort** means pain, uneasiness, or distress.
*Michelle's sprained wrist gave her much **discomfort** during the match.*

## Discover, invent

**Discover** means to find something already in existence, but unknown.
*Try to **discover** the events that have shaped this great country of ours.*

**Invent** means to create something new.
*Edison did not **invent** the light bulb; the inventor was Joseph Swan.*

## Discreet, discrete

**Discreet** means to be prudent or show good judgment.
*When arranging Becky's party, be **discreet**; we want to surprise her.*

**Discrete** means separate or distinct.
*The conversion process consists of five **discrete** steps.*

## Discrepancy, disparity

**Discrepancy** means a difference between facts or claims.
*A **discrepancy** exists between the appraised value and the asking price.*

**Disparity** means inequality or difference in some respect.
*We found a big **disparity** between their ideals and their actions.*

## Disenfranchise, disfranchise

**Disfranchise** is preferred in American usage.

## Disinformation, misinformation

**Disinformation** refers to deliberately misleading information.
*The competition gave us **disinformation** about their new products.*

**Misinformation** refers to incorrect information.
*The paper printed **misinformation** about the group's concert dates.*

## Disingenuous, ingenious, ingenuous

**Disingenuous** means devious, dishonest, or pretending.
*He's being rather **disingenuous**, saying nothing is wrong with the house.*

**Ingenious** means clever, imaginative, or original.
*Art developed an **ingenious** solution to the hardware problem.*

**Ingenuous** means candid, honest, or innocent.
*Louise and Rick have an open, **ingenuous** manner that people like.*

## Disinterested, uninterested

**Disinterested** means impartial, neutral, objective, or unbiased.
*We chose Maria as a* ***disinterested*** *third party to make the decision.*

**Uninterested** means bored, indifferent, or simply not interested.
*Despite Jim's enthusiasm, his boss remains* ***uninterested*** *in the project.*

## Disorganized, unorganized

**Disorganized** means thrown into disorder or disarray.
*We have never seen a dormitory room so* ***disorganized*** *and untidy.*

**Unorganized** means not yet organized or lacking order.
*Given the league started 4 years ago, it still appears* ***unorganized.***

## Disorientated, disoriented

**Disoriented**, meaning to feel displaced, is the preferred spelling.
*Lori and Damian felt groggy and* ***disoriented*** *after their long flight.*

## Disparage, disparate

**Disparage** means to criticize or belittle someone.
*Tom's comment was in no way meant to* ***disparage*** *a nice guy like Ed.*

**Disparate** means fundamentally different or distinct in quality or kind.
*The community event for charity brought many* ***disparate*** *people together.*

## Dispense with, dispose of

**Dispense with** means to do without something.
*We would like to **dispense with** all the unnecessary paperwork.*

**Dispose of** means to get rid of something.
*Where can I **dispose of** the used oil and antifreeze?*

## Displace, misplace

**Displace** means to shift, change, or move the position of something.
*The raging floods **displaced** many residents for weeks.*

**Misplace** means to put in a wrong place or lose something.
*It's easy to **misplace** or forget a punctuation mark in a long sentence.*

## Dissatisfied, unsatisfied

Both these adjectives generally relate to being not satisfied; however, each word has a special meaning.

**Dissatisfied** usually describes people or animals.
*The couple is **dissatisfied** with the food and service at this restaurant.*

**Unsatisfied** usually relates to inanimate things.
*They have an **unsatisfied** court judgment against the other party.*

## Dissect, bisect

*See entry for **Bisect, dissect.***

## Distinct, distinctive

**Distinct** means clearly apparent, discrete, separate, or obvious.
*A **distinct** improvement in giving helped many poor families last year.*

**Distinctive** means distinguished or standing out as being different.
*Justin Hayward's **distinctive** voice has won the Moody Blues many fans.*

## Diversity, adversity

*See entry for **Adversity, diversity.***

## Divert, avert

*See entry for **Avert, avoid, divert.***

## Dogmatic, pragmatic

**Dogmatic** means arrogantly authoritative or overbearing.
*His **dogmatic** and demanding personality did not fit in well with us.*

**Pragmatic** means to take a practical approach.
*Pat offered us a **pragmatic** way for getting the work done by 5 p.m.*

## Dominant, dominate, domineer

**Dominant** means commanding or controlling over all others.
*The body naturally responds to the **dominant** eye for sight.*

**Dominate** means to control, govern, or regulate.
*Their software **dominates** the financial services industry.*

**Domineer** means to exercise arbitrary or overbearing control.
*The strong will of a few can easily **domineer** a community.*

## DOS operating system

Redundancy. **DOS** means *Disk Operating System*. Just use **DOS**.

## Dough, batter

*See entry for **Batter, dough**.*

## Douse, dowse

**Douse** means to extinguish or wet thoroughly.
*The firefighters **doused** the flames with water most of the night.*

**Dowse** means to look for water or minerals with a divining rod.
*It was not uncommon for the pioneers to **dowse** for water on the trail.*

## Downfall, drawback

**Downfall** refers to something that causes destruction.
*The Russian Revolution of 1917 led to the **downfall** of Czar Nicholas II.*

**Drawback** refers to just a flaw or problem of some kind.
*Marty's plan to camp in the park has one **drawback**: too many gnats.*

## Downward, downwards

**Downward** is preferred in American usage.

## DSL line

Redundancy. **DSL** means *Digital Subscriber Line.* Just use **DSL.**

## Dual, duel

**Dual** refers to two things.
*After you install the **dual** carburetors, open the throttle about half way.*

**Duel** refers to a formal battle or contest intended to settle a dispute.
*"**Duel** of the Titans" is a film based on the Romulus and Remus legend.*

## Due to, because of

*See entry for **Because of, due to.***

## DVD disc

Redundancy. **DVD** means *Digital Video* (or *Versatile*) *Disc.* Just use **DVD.**

# E

"*Every word was once a poem.*" — Ralph Waldo Emerson

## Each other, one another

**Each other** refers to two persons or things.
*No doubt, their relationship confirms they love* ***each other.***

**One another** refers to more than two persons or things.
*Videoconferencing allows people to see as well as hear* ***one another.***

## Eager, anxious

*See entry for* ***Anxious, eager.***

## Eastward, eastwards

**Eastward** is preferred in American usage.

## Eclectic, esoteric, exoteric

**Eclectic** means the best of something from many sources.
*With music from Bach to the Beatles, the concert was definitely* ***eclectic.***

**Esoteric** means confined to or understood by just a few people.
*The author's* ***esoteric*** *use of language can deter the average reader.*

**Exoteric** means not confined to a particular group but suitable for all.
*She designs and writes books with an* ***exoteric*** *audience in mind.*

## Ecology, environment

**Ecology** refers to relationships between organisms and their environment.
*This semester the students are studying the* ***ecology*** *of the African jungle.*

**Environment** refers to conditions that surround an organism.
*Countries are concerned that nuclear waste can hurt the* ***environment****.*

## Economic, economical

**Economic** refers to the economy, material wealth, or financial reward.
*An* ***economic*** *recovery is predicted for early next year.*
*We sold our vacation house strictly for* ***economic*** *reasons.*
*It is not* ***economic*** *to keep both stores operating next year.*

**Economical** refers to being not wasteful.
*Our new car is more* ***economical*** *on gas than any car we've owned.*

## Eerie, aerie, airy

*See entry for* ***Aerie, airy, eerie.***

## Effect, affect

*See entry for* ***Affect, effect.***

## Effective, efficacious, efficient

**Effective** means impressive, operative, or producing the desired effect.
*Tony Bennett put on an* ***effective*** *performance at Saratoga last summer.*

*The new fiscal calendar is **effective** as of today.*
*The talks were **effective** in gaining peace within a few days.*

**Efficacious** means having the power to achieve the desired effect.
*The doctor applied an **efficacious** remedy to the patient.*

**Efficient** means achieving results through a good use of resources.
*Some fuel **efficient** cars can get 60 miles to a gallon of gas.*

## Effluent, affluent

*See entry for **Affluent, effluent.***

## EIN number

Redundancy. **EIN** means *Employer Identification Number.* Just use **EIN**.

## Either, neither

**Either** means one or the other of two.
*We can ride in **either** Dick's new pickup truck or my old car.*

**Neither** means not one or the other of two.
*Under the new agreement, **neither** party may sell or transfer its rights.*

## Elapse, lapse

**Elapse** means to pass by or slip away.
*How much time **elapses** before the officials make a decision?*

**Lapse** means to drift, to discontinue, or to terminate.
*The magazine subscription* ***lapses*** *unless you renew it soon.*

## Elegy, eulogy

**Elegy** refers to a poem of lament or praise for a dead person.
*Walt Whitman wrote a famous* ***elegy*** *on the death of President Lincoln.*

**Eulogy** refers to speech or writing in praise of a person, thing, or event.
*Earl Spencer wrote a moving* ***eulogy*** *to his sister, Princess Diana.*

## Elicit, illicit

**Elicit** means to bring out or draw forth.
*The band's performances always* ***elicit*** *praise from the critics.*

**Illicit** means unlawful or prohibited.
*The commission confronted the investment firm for its* ***illicit*** *activities.*

## Elude, allude, refer

*See entry for* ***Allude, elude, refer****.*

## Elusive, illusive

**Elusive** means hard to catch, grasp, or define.
*Director Stanley Kubrick remained an* ***elusive*** *figure to the press.*

**Illusive** means deceptive or unreal.
*Magician David Copperfield amazes audiences with his* ***illusive*** *tricks.*

## Embargo, boycott

*See entry for* ***Boycott, embargo.***

## Emend, amend

*See entry for* ***Amend, emend.***

## Emerge, immerge, immerse

**Emerge** means to come out, rise up, or come forth.
*It looks like Sara* ***emerges*** *as the winner after all.*

**Immerge** and **immerse** mean to plunge into or submerge.
***Immerge*** *(****immerse****) the knee in ice to minimize the swelling.*

## Emigrant, immigrant, migrant

**Emigrant** is one who leaves one's native country to settle in another.
*The* ***emigrants*** *spent a few weeks aboard ship before landing in Maine.*

**Immigrant** is one who enters and settles in a new country.
*Many* ***immigrants*** *are looking for jobs in the larger cities.*

**Migrant** is one who travels about, especially in search of work.
*The* ***migrants*** *are working in the apple orchards of New York.*

## Eminent, immanent, imminent

**Eminent** means distinguished, famous, outstanding, or prominent.
***Eminent** scientists are expressing serious concerns for the coral reefs.*

**Immanent** means inherent, indwelling, or present within the universe.
*The theologian suggests that God is **immanent** in all life forms.*

**Imminent** means about to happen or threatening.
*The bidders tell us the government contract award is **imminent**.*

## Empathy, sympathy

**Empathy** is being able to relate to someone.
*Singer Harry Chapin always felt a great sense of **empathy** for the hungry.*

**Sympathy** is feeling sorry for someone.
*The club conveyed its deepest **sympathy** with a beautiful gift basket.*

## Emulate, simulate

**Emulate** means to strive to equal or excel, usually through imitation.
*The new TV comedy tried to **emulate** the premise of another show.*

**Simulate** means to take on the appearance or form of something.
*The testing lab can **simulate** an actual aircraft landing.*

## En route, on route

**En route**, meaning along the way, is the correct phrase.
*The package is **en route** directly from the factory.*

## Enclose, inclose

**Enclose** is preferred in American usage.
*Please **enclose** your latest resume with the job application.*

## Endemic, epidemic

**Endemic** means peculiar to a given country or people.
*The fish are **endemic** to the native waters of the Hawaiian Islands.*

**Epidemic** means breaking out suddenly and affecting many people.
*The foot and mouth **epidemic** still exists in some areas.*

## Endless, innumerable

**Endless** means without end, boundless, or interminable.
*Many of us wish all our summers were **endless**.*

**Innumerable** means too many to count (countless).
*The miracles of healing are among the **innumerable** gifts of God.*

## Enervate, invigorate

**Enervate** means to drain energy or weaken something.
*The hot and humid weather **enervated** all of us.*

**Invigorate** means to be energized by something.
*The coach's pep talk at halftime **invigorated** Harry and Greg.*

## Enormity, enormousness

**Enormity** means immensely outrageous or wicked.
*The **enormity** of the defendant's crimes surprised the jury.*

**Enormousness** means much larger than expected.
*The **enormousness** of the facility amazed the people.*

## Enough, ample

*See entry for **Ample, enough.***

## Enquire, inquire

**Inquire** is the preferred spelling, but either one is acceptable.

## Ensure, assure, insure

*See entry for **Assure, ensure, insure.***

## Enthral, enthrall

**Enthrall**, meaning to captivate, is preferred in American usage.
*Susan's second novel **enthralled** us more than her first novel.*

## Enthused, enthusiastic

**Enthused** is not popular with writing authorities. Prefer **enthusiastic.**
*The students are **enthusiastic** (not **enthused**) about the new school.*

## Entitled, titled

**Entitled** means to have the right to something.
*Because Ellen is the songwriter, she is* ***entitled*** *to the music royalties.*

**Titled** refers to the name of a publication, speech, or musical piece.
*Their first musical piece this evening is* ***titled,*** *"The Voice."*

## Entomology, etymology

**Entomology** is the study of insects. **Etymology** is the study of word origins.

## Entrust, intrust

**Entrust** is preferred in American usage.
*They* ***entrust*** *our firm with the management of their financial affairs.*

## Enunciate, annunciate

*See entry for* ***Annunciate, enunciate.***

## Enure, inure

**Inure**, meaning to get used to something undesirable, is preferred in American usage.
*Considering our remote site, we are* ***inured*** *to frequent power outages.*

## Envelop, envelope

**Envelop**, a verb, means to enclose, surround, or wrap something.
*The baby is **enveloped** in a blanket to keep warm.*

**Envelope**, a noun, is the flat paper container for papers.
*The invitation arrived in a plain white **envelope**.*

## Enviable, envious

**Enviable** means worthy of envy.
*John Glenn has an **enviable** place in the history of space travel.*

**Envious** means showing envy toward one's success or good fortune.
*Some astronauts are **envious** of John Glenn's mark on space travel.*

## Epigram, epigraph, epitaph, epithet

**Epigram** is a short humorous saying.
*Oscar Wilde wrote the **epigram**: "I can resist everything except temptation."*

**Epigraph** is a brief quotation at the beginning of a book or an inscription on a monument, statue, or building.
*The **epigraph** to E. M. Forster's novel* "Howards End" *is 'Only connect!'.*

**Epitaph** is a tribute to a dead person inscribed on a gravestone.
*In his **epitaph** to his son, Vernon Presley wrote: "He revolutionized the field of music and received its highest awards."*

**Epithet** is a short descriptive word or phrase applied to someone.
*Because of his bravery, Richard Coeur de Lion earned the* ***epithet*** *'Lionheart'.*

## Equable, equitable

**Equable** means unvarying, agreeable, or steady.
*Ireland's* ***equable*** *climate is due largely to being so close to the sea.*

**Equitable** means impartial, fair, or reasonable.
*The club gave an* ***equitable*** *distribution of gifts to the local charities.*

## Equipment, equipments

Use **equipment. Equipments** is not a word.

## Equivocably, equivocally

**Equivocably** is not a word.

## Erasable, irascible

**Erasable** means capable of being rubbed out or removed.
*You need* ***erasable*** *markers for that white board.*

**Irascible** means easily provoked, angered, or disagreeable.
*After months of being unemployed, he became* ***irascible*** *to everyone.*

## Erode, corrode

*See entry for* ***Corrode, erode.***

## Errant, arrant

*See entry for **Arrant, errant.***

## Eruption, irruption

**Eruption** refers to a violent outburst or discharge of material.
*The **eruption** of Mount Vesuvius destroyed Pompei in 79 AD.*

**Irruption** refers to an increase, such as in population.
*An **irruption** of winter finches from Canada's north woods is expected.*

## Especially, specially

**Especially** means particularly or standing apart from all the rest.
*The air quality in the Adirondack Mountains is **especially** refreshing.*

**Specially** means for a specific purpose or reason.
*Those students were **specially** chosen for their artistic talents.*

## Essay, assay

*See entry for **Assay, essay.***

## EST time

Redundancy. **EST** means *Eastern Standard Time*. Just use **EST**.

## Estimated ETA

Redundancy. **ETA** means *Estimated Time of Arrival.* Just use **ETA**.

## Eternal, everlasting

**Eternal** refers to something that is without beginning or end.
***Eternal** peace and happiness are the wishes of many people.*

**Everlasting** refers to something that goes on forever.
*The natural beauty and splendor of Lake Tahoe is **everlasting**.*

## Eternity, affinity, infinity

*See entry for **Affinity, eternity, infinity**.*

## Euphemism, euphuism

**Euphemism** is a substitute word or phrase that is less offensive to people.
*The phrase "previously owned" is a **euphemism** for "used".*

**Euphuism** is an old literary term for an elegant or pretentious literary style.
*His plain writing style is in direct contrast to the ornate style of **euphuism**.*

## Ever so often, every so often

**Ever so often** means frequently, and **every so often** means occasionally.
*Please be sure to check back (**ever so often**,* or ***every so often**) for news.*

## Every body, everybody

**Every body** means every person or thing without an exception.
***Every body** on the team will try to improve his or her golf swing.*

**Everybody** means all the people.
*Everybody on the team knows Sam has the best golf swing.*

## Every day, everyday

**Every day** means each day without an exception.
*We try to back up our hard drive* ***every day.***

**Everyday** means ordinary, common, or not unusual.
*Problems are a natural* ***everyday*** *occurrence of life.*

## Every one, everyone

**Every one** means every person or thing without an exception.
*The deer ate* ***every one*** *of the shrubs last winter.*

**Everyone** means all the people.
*Is* ***everyone*** *ready to begin the test?*

## Evidence, proof

**Evidence** is supporting information that helps to form a conclusion.
*Scientists have* ***evidence*** *that suggests life could have existed on Mars.*

**Proof** is factual evidence that helps establish truth and remove doubt.
*His attorney had no problem uncovering* ***proof*** *of Bruce's innocence.*

## Evince, evoke, invoke

**Evince** means to exhibit or show something clearly.
*Paul McCartney* ***evinced*** *an amazing talent for music as a child.*

**Evoke** means to bring out something hidden or unexpressed.
*The music* **evoked** *many good memories of Molly's college days.*

**Invoke** means to call upon for help or to activate.
*The defendant* **invoked** *the Fifth Amendment during the trial.*
*You can* **invoke** *that command by pressing the Enter key twice.*

## Exalt, exult

**Exalt** means to raise, praise, or elevate a person or thing.
*Let us* **exalt** *the brilliance of your achievements and ideas.*

**Exult** means to rejoice greatly.
*The professor* **exulted** *at the chance to become department chairman.*

## Exceed, accede, concede

*See entry for* ***Accede, concede, exceed.***

## Except, accept

*See entry for* ***Accept, except.***

## Exceptionable, exceptional

**Exceptionable** means objectionable, offensive, or debatable.
*We found their crude language and conduct quite* **exceptionable.**
*The court made some* **exceptionable** *and unpopular decisions last year.*

**Exceptional** means uncommon, unusual, or extraordinary.
*That student has an **exceptional** memory for small details.*

## Excess, access

*See entry for **Access, excess.***

## Expand, expend

**Expand** means to increase something.
*The company's healthcare business **expanded** by 50 percent last year.*

**Expend** means to lay out or spend.
*The company **expended** most of its effort to increase healthcare sales.*

## Expatiate, expiate

**Expatiate** means to write or speak at great length.
*That company likes to **expatiate** in great detail about their products.*

**Expiate** means to atone or make amends for something.
*He wanted to **expiate** in some way the guilt he felt all those years.*

## Expect, anticipate

*See entry for **Anticipate, expect.***

## Expedient, expeditious

**Expedient** means serving to promote or advance one's own interest.
*It is **expedient** for him to start his re-election campaign early.*

**Expeditious** means acting with speed and efficiency.
*The fund transfer must be done by the most **expeditious** means.*

## Explicit, implicit

**Explicit** means clearly defined or stated.
*Their comments about the film are quite **explicit** as well as surprising.*

**Implicit** means implied or understood but not expressed.
*We have an **implicit** understanding with the building contractor.*

## Extant, extent

**Extant** means still existing.
*Few copies of Frank Sinatra's first album are **extant**.*

**Extent** means the measure of or the limit of something.
*We do not know the **extent** of the research done on the disease.*

## Extrapolate, interpolate

**Extrapolate** means to estimate or predict from known information.
*We can **extrapolate** from your findings and determine an estimate.*

**Interpolate** means to insert or introduce between other parts or things. *The reviewer's comments to the text are **interpolated** in the margins.*

# F

*"All the fun's in how you say a thing."* — Robert Frost

## Facetious, factious, factitious

**Facetious** means humorous or amusing.
*Colleen was just being **facetious** with her stories and meant no harm.*

**Factious** means causing internal dissension or opposition.
*A **factious** attitude can hinder any workplace.*

**Factitious** means artificial or unnatural.
*Speculation probably caused the **factitious** value of those stocks.*
*The doctor ruled out either a malingering or a **factitious** disorder.*

## Facilitate, felicitate

**Facilitate** means to make easier.
*Some spell checkers also try to **facilitate** grammatical errors in text.*

**Felicitate** means to congratulate or make happy.
*I **felicitate** you on your continued generosity and thoughtfulness.*

## Faint, feign, feint

**Faint** refers to being dizzy, lacking clarity, or lacking brightness.
*She felt quite **faint** after the rigorous workout in the gym.*
*He has a **faint** recollection of what actually happened last night.*
*The sun cast a **faint** shadow on the house at day's end.*

**Feign** refers to giving a false appearance.
*In the driving class, one student was asked to **feign** an injury.*

**Feint** refers to a pretended punch in boxing.
*Muhammad Ali used many **feints** in the ring against his opponents.*

## Famous, infamous, notorious

**Famous** means to be widely known.
*Tom Clancy, the **famous** author, autographed Jim and Tom's books.*

**Infamous** and **notorious** mean widely known and unfavorably regarded.
*His gambling success made him **infamous (notorious)** at the casinos.*

## FAQ question

Redundancy. **FAQ** means *Frequently Asked Question.* Just use **FAQ.**

## Farther, further

**Farther** refers to a physical distance.
*Do not place the unit **farther** than 10 feet from the house.*

**Further** refers to a greater degree or extent.
*Any **further** delay in the decision could be a problem.*

## Fatal, fateful

**Fatal** refers to causing death, destruction, or ruin.
*By heeding the advice of others, the group made a **fatal** mistake.*

**Fateful** refers to one's destiny.
*Gordon Lightfoot wrote about the Edmund Fitzgerald's* ***fateful*** *voyage.*

## Father-in-laws, fathers-in-law

**Fathers-in-law** is the correct phrase.

## Faun, fawn

**Faun** is a wild creature of Roman legend that is part man and part goat.
*The* ***faun*** *is a disciple of the god Faunus.*

**Fawn** is a young deer usually less than a year old.
*If you see a* ***fawn*** *alone, a doe is likely nearby.*

## Faze, phase

**Faze** means to disrupt or disturb.
*The economic slowdown did not* ***faze*** *their business at all.*

**Phase** means to carry out or conduct.
*Mike is going to* ***phase*** *in the new accounting procedures gradually.*

## Fervent, fervid

**Fervent** means passionate or warm.
*It is our* ***fervent*** *wish that Bob quickly recover from his illness.*

**Fervid** means impassioned or extremely hot.
*Peggy and Joe have a* ***fervid*** *dislike for cold climates.*
*Diane and Fred endured the* ***fervid*** *temperatures of the tropical climate.*

## Fever, temperature

A **fever** is a **temperature** higher than 98.6° F.

## Fewer, less, lest

**Fewer** refers to a number of individual persons or things.
***Fewer** than 100 members responded to the appeal.*

**Less** refers to quantity or how much.
*Because of the drought, the fields are producing **less** sugar this year.*

Note: If the number is only *one*, use **less.**
*One **less** person attended the meeting.*

**Lest** means for fear that.
***Lest** we forget, he did a nice job last time and deserves recognition.*

## Fiancé, fiancée

**Fiancé** is a man engaged to be married. **Fiancée** is a woman engaged to be married.

## Fictional, fictitious

**Fictional** refers to fiction.
*The **fictional** character Yoda is in the film "The Empire Strikes Back."*

**Fictitious** refers to being imaginary or nonexistent.
*I can conduct business in this state under an assumed or **fictitious** name.*

## Figuratively, literally

**Figuratively** means metaphorically or symbolically.
*__Figuratively__ speaking, his idea is turning the world of business on edge.*

**Literally** means following the exact meanings of the words.
*Several thoughtful volunteers **literally** built that house in 1 month.*

## Flagrant, blatant

*See entry for **Blatant, flagrant.***

## Flammable, inflammable, nonflammable

**Flammable** and **inflammable** are synonyms meaning burnable.
*It's dangerous to light a match near a **flammable** (**inflammable**) liquid.*

**Nonflammable** means not flammable or not easily ignited.
*Trichlorofluoro methane is a colorless, **nonflammable** gas.*

## Flaunt, flout

**Flaunt** means to display boastfully or show off something.
*They **flaunt** their superior wisdom and status in the faces of others.*

**Flout** means to ignore or show disrespect for something.
*In showing a lack of respect, they **flout** the most basic of rules.*

## Flotsam, jetsam

**Flotsam** is floating cargo or wreckage following a shipwreck.
*The **flotsam** floated for weeks, long after the ship sank.*

**Jetsam** is something thrown overboard to lighten a ship in distress.
*The **jetsam** consisted of many cartons containing canned food.*

## Flounder, founder

**Flounder** means to behave awkwardly or move in a clumsy way.
*The key witness **floundered** during her testimony.*
*Art **floundered** a few minutes on the ice before gaining his balance.*

**Founder** means to sink or collapse.
*On its approach, the small ship struck a rock and quickly **foundered.***
*The prosecutor's case **foundered** after her key witness's testimony.*

## Forbear, forebear

**Forbear**, a verb, means to abstain or refrain from something.
*We **forbear** from making any negative comments toward them.*

**Forebear**, a noun, means an ancestor.
*My **forebear** was a humorous person who enjoyed telling many jokes.*

## Forbid, prohibit

Both these verbs mean refusing to allow something.

**Forbid** is usually followed by an infinitive or an *ing* form and never takes *from*.
*Both the parents and grandparents **forbid** him to quit school.*
*Their coach **forbid** them missing any of the Saturday practices.*

**Prohibit** is usually followed by the word *from* and an *ing* form.
*The college **prohibits** students from cutting classes.*

## Forbidding, foreboding

**Forbidding** means unpleasant or to make progress or passage difficult.
*He gave us a **forbidding** look when we asked about our repair bill.*
*The **forbidding** bottle neck of traffic made us late for the game.*

**Foreboding** means a premonition about something (usually negative).
*They had a **foreboding** the weather would not cooperate this vacation.*

## Forceful, forcible

**Forceful** means powerful, vigorous, or effective.
*His **forceful** personality dominates much of the interview.*

**Forcible** means exercising by force or violence.
*By breaking the lock, the police made a **forcible** entry into the house.*

## Forego, forgo

**Forego** means to go before in place or time.
*Barb's competent work and excellent reputation always **foregoes** her.*
*It is no longer a **foregone** conclusion that John will retire this year.*

**Forgo** means to give up, do without, or relinquish.
*To compete in running races, you should **forgo** fatty foods.*

## Foreword, preface

The **foreword** of a book is an introductory note not written by the author. The **preface** is a statement written by the author about the book's objective or purpose.

## Formally, formerly

**Formally** means in a traditional or formal manner.
*Celeste and Daniel are **formally** dressed for the occasion.*

**Formerly** means in the past or happened before.
*Jesse Ventura was **formerly** known as "The Body" in pro wrestling.*

## Former, latter

**Former** refers to the first of two and **latter** the second of two (or last of many). Note that when you use these words, the reader (or listener) must remember what was written (or said). This can sometimes be annoying, and you might want to reconsider using these words.

## Fortuitous, fortunate

**Fortuitous** means happening by chance or random.
*The software sales caused a **fortuitous** rise in needed revenue.*

**Fortunate** means being lucky or having good fortune.
*Maggie is **fortunate** in that her unemployment lasted just a few months.*

## Forward, forwards

**Forward** means to be toward the front or to send on to someone.
*Please step **forward** when your name is called.*
*Please **forward** the bill to the customer's new home address.*

**Forwards** is not preferred in American usage. Use **forward** instead.

## Fragment, fragmentary

**Fragment** refers to a small part detached from something.
*That meteorite may be a **fragment** of a primitive asteroid.*

**Fragmentary** refers to disconnected or incomplete parts.
***Fragmentary** remains usually help identify dinosaurs.*

## Frantically, franticly

**Frantically** is preferred in American usage.

## Free, freely

**Free**, an adverb, means without charge.
*Faculty and students are admitted to the game **free**.*

**Freely**, an adverb, means in a free manner or without any restrictions.
*Faculty and students are admitted to the game **freely**.*

## Freeze, frieze

**Freeze** means to change from a liquid into a solid, to stop, or to exclude.
*Water **freezes** at 32° Fahrenheit.*
*My computer usually **freezes** when I access the Internet.*
*The new park fees could **freeze** out the lower income families.*

**Frieze** refers to an ornament.
*A **frieze** that shows the history of the city is hung in the hallway.*

## Friend, acquaintance

*See entry for **Acquaintance, friend.***

## Frontward, frontwards

**Frontward** is preferred in American usage.

## FSLIC corporation

Redundancy. **FSLIC** means *Federal Savings and Loan Insurance Corporation*. Just use **FSLIC.**

## Funeral, funerary, funereal

**Funeral** refers to the service held for a dead person.
*The NFDA is the largest **funeral** service organization in the world.*

**Funerary** means associated with burial.
*It remains uncertain about the **funerary** beliefs during the Old Kingdom.*

**Funereal** means like a funeral, suggestive of death, gloomy, or sad.
*The atmosphere is very somber, serious, and **funereal.***

# G

"*When ideas fail, words come in very handy.*" — Johann Wolfgang von Goethe

## Gabardine, gaberdine

**Gabardine**, a durable fabric with a twill weave, is preferred in American usage.
*Daniel is wearing his blue **gabardine** dress slacks to the interview.*

## Gaff, gaffe

**Gaff** is an iron hook attached to a pole usually used to grab large fish.
*The seaman uses a **gaff** to catch the large tuna.*

**Gaffe** is a social error, blunder, or indiscreet remark (faux pas).
*I made a **gaffe** by mispronouncing my supervisor's last name.*

## Gamble, gambol

**Gamble** means to risk, chance, or bet on something.
*I wouldn't **gamble** on the weather cooperating for the Strawberry Festival.*

To **gambol** means to leap and skip about playfully.
*The children are joyfully **gamboling** around the school yard.*

## Genial, congenial, congenital

*See entry for **Congenial, congenital, genial.***

## Genius, genus

**Genius** is a person with exceptional ability, intelligence, or talent.
*Surprisingly, Albert Einstein was not considered a boy* ***genius.***

**Genus** is a category, class, or type in taxonomy.
*The museum lists all plant pictures in the gallery by* ***genus*** *and species.*

## Gibe, jibe

**Gibe** means to jeer, mock, or tease at a person.
*Eric sometimes* ***gibes*** *him about his unfortunate four-putt green.*

**Jibe** means to agree with something.
*Your independent audit* ***jibes*** *well with the accounting firm's numbers.*

## Gild, guild

**Gild** means to cover with a golden appearance.
*The beautiful Canadian sunset* ***gilded*** *the grass in the valley.*

**Guild** refers to an association of trades people.
*Steven Spielberg is a member of the Directors* ***Guild*** *of America.*

## Gilt, guilt

**Gilt**, as an adjective, means covered with gold (from the verb **gild**).
*She is wearing an elaborate* ***gilt*** *necklace to the party.*

**Gilt**, as a noun, refers to a thin gold covering or layer.
*Because of age, much of the* ***gilt*** *has worn away from the necklace.*

**Guilt**, a noun, means being responsible for a wrongdoing or error.
*The seminar includes the topics of **guilt** and forgiveness.*

## Gist, jest

**Gist** refers to the central idea of something.
*I understand the **gist** of what Tommy is trying to say.*

**Jest** refers to making a joke.
*My comments are not intended to be negative, but rather spoken in **jest**.*

## Glutton, gourmand, gourmet

**Glutton** refers to someone who eats or drinks to excess, or someone who has a great capacity for enduring something.
*"I am not a **glutton**. I am an explorer of food."* — Erma Bombeck
*You must be a **glutton** for pain to run another marathon.*

**Gourmand** refers to someone who is very fond of food and drink.
*Brian is quite a **gourmand**, and never skimps in his shopping cart.*

**Gourmet** refers to a connoisseur of food and drink.
*Being a **gourmet** is one prerequisite for being a TV cooking expert.*

## GMT time

Redundancy. **GMT** means *Greenwich Mean Time*. Just use **GMT**.

## Gone, went

**Gone** must always be preceded by 1 of the 23 auxiliary (or helping) verbs (*are, was, were, have,* and others). **Went** never takes an auxiliary (or helping) verb.

*I should* ***have gone*** *to college when I had the chance.*
*I* ***went*** *to college immediately after high school.*

Note: The 23 auxiliary (or helping) verbs are: *am, are, be, being, been, can, could, did, do, does, had, has, have, is, may, might, must, shall, should, was, were, will,* and *would.*

## Good, well

**Good** is an adjective.
*Debbie has always been a* ***good*** *elementary teacher.*

**Well** can be an adjective (when referring to one's health) or an adverb.
*A few of the students do not look* ***well*** *today.*
*Debbie has always taught the students* ***well.***

## Gorilla, guerrilla

**Gorilla** refers to a large ape. **Guerrilla** refers to a member (soldier) of an independent armed resistance force.

## Graduated, graduated from

**Graduated from** is the correct phrase.
*I* ***graduated from*** *the State University at Albany in 1974.*

## Grammar, syntax

**Grammar** is the complete study of a language (pronunciations, meanings, or history). **Syntax** is a part of grammar that deals with how words form phrases, clauses, and sentences.

## Grateful, gratified, gratuitous

**Grateful** means to feel gratitude for an action.
*Many parents are **grateful** for the principal's intervention.*

**Gratified** means to give pleasure or satisfy.
*Walter's achievements in high school **gratified** his parents.*

**Gratuitous** means free, unjustified, or unwanted.
*The guidance office gave **gratuitous** advice on college scholarships.*

## GRE exam

Redundancy. **GRE** means *Graduate Record Exam*. Just use **GRE**.

## Grisly, gristly, grizzled, grizzly

**Grisly** means ghastly or gruesome.
*The prosecutor painted a **grisly** picture of the event to the jurors.*

**Gristly** means composed of or containing gristle.
*The children gave the dog the **gristly** end to chew.*

**Grizzled** means partly gray or streaked with gray.
*Our leader today is a **grizzled** old veteran of many mountain climbs.*

**Grizzly** is a bear.
*The **grizzly** bear is perhaps the greatest symbol of the wilderness.*

## Guarantee, guaranty

**Guarantee**, a noun or a verb, means agreement, assurance, or security.
*The car dealer offers an exceptional **guarantee** on the used vehicle.*
*The car dealer **guaranteed** the used vehicle for 1 year.*

**Guaranty**, a noun, also means agreement, assurance, or security.
*The car dealer's record is a **guaranty** of his honesty with customers.*

# H

*"A word is not a crystal, transparent and unchanging. It is the skin of living thought."* — Oliver Wendell Holmes, Jr.

## Habitant, habitat

**Habitant** means an inhabitant (person or animal).
*Few **habitants** of that area escaped the severe winter storms.*

**Habitat** means the native environment of a person, animal, or plant.
*Johnny supports organizations that conserve **habitat** for the wildlife.*

## Hanged, hung

**Hanged** means executed by hanging.
*The five conspirators in the Lincoln assassination were **hanged**.*

**Hung** means suspended.
*The Christmas stockings are **hung** by the chimney with care.*

Note: Some writing authorities still accept **hung** as meaning to execute.

## Hate, despise

*See entry for **Despise, hate**.*

## Healthful, healthy

**Healthful** means conducive to good health.
*We live in upstate because of its **healthful** climate and beautiful scenery.*

**Healthy** means possessing good health.
*Diet, exercise, and plenty of rest keep them **healthy** and energetic.*

Memory hook: Things are **healthful**; people and animals are **healthy**.

## Height, heighth

The correct spelling is **height**.

## Hence, thence, whence

**Hence** means from here, from now, or thus.
*Two years **hence** and this entire episode will be forgotten by all.*
*It is going to rain, **hence** the high humidity and clouds.*

**Thence** means from that time or from that place.
*We flew to Raleigh and **thence** to Dallas on our way back.*

**Whence** (an old word) means from what place, source, or cause.
***Whence** came all this valuable information?*

## Herbivorous, carnivorous, omnivorous

*See entry for **Carnivorous, herbivorous, omnivorous.***

## Historic, historical

**Historic** means when something is important or memorable.
*The opening of the new wing is a **historic** occasion for the hospital.*

**Historical** means concerned with or relating to history.
*Margaret Mitchell's "Gone with the Wind" is a **historical** novel.*

## HIV virus

Redundancy. **HIV** means *Human Immunodeficiency Virus.* Just use **HIV**.

## Hoard, horde

**Hoard** refers to a hidden find or cache.
*Jim found a **hoard** of Roman coins with his metal detector.*

**Horde** refers to a crowd or throng.
*We ran into a **horde** of mosquitoes at last night's softball game.*

## Home, house

**Home** refers to intangible things (emotions) within a dwelling.
*It's obvious they are all being raised in a very happy **home**.*

**House** refers to a structure that can be built, bought, or sold.
*The real estate broker just put their **house** on the market.*

## Home in on, hone in on

**Home in on** is the correct phrase.
*With that obvious clue, we can* ***home in on*** *the answer.*

## Homographs, homophones

**Homographs** are words spelled alike but different in meaning and pronunciation (noun *project* vs. the verb *project*).

**Homophones** are words pronounced alike but different in spelling and meaning (*their, there* and *real, reel*).

## How ever, however

**How ever** is used for emphasis.
***How ever*** *did you get front row seats for the concert?*

**However** means in whatever manner or nevertheless.
***However*** *the board decides, we probably should just accept it.*
***However,*** *the board should make a decision on the matter soon.*

## HTML language

Redundancy. HTML means *HyperText Markup Language*. Just use HTML.

## Hue, shade, tint

**Hue** is a color's intensity.
**Shade** is a slightly darker color produced by a pigment.
**Tint** is a pale variation of a color.

## Hurdle, hurtle

**Hurdle** refers to a difficulty or obstacle.
*The Health Care Bill cleared a big* ***hurdle*** *in the Senate yesterday.*

**Hurtle** means to move with great speed or to go violently.
*Many baby boomers are* ***hurtling*** *toward their retirement age.*
*The tornado sent debris* ***hurtling*** *all over the community.*

## Hurricane, typhoon

A **hurricane** is a severe tropical storm that starts east of the International Date Line (Atlantic Ocean, Caribbean Sea, or Gulf of Mexico). A **typhoon** is a severe tropical storm that starts west of the International Date Line (Pacific Ocean or China Sea).

## Hypercritical, hypocritical

**Hypercritical** means over critical, excessively exact, or picky.
*Gene's* ***hypercritical*** *movie review has the film's producers concerned.*

**Hypocritical** means two-faced or practicing hypocrisy.
*It may be* ***hypocritical*** *of the newspaper to criticize the paparazzi.*

# I

*"Half my life is an act of revision."* — John Irving

## ICU unit

Redundancy. **ICU** means *Intensive Care Unit.* Just use **ICU.**

## Ignorant, stupid

**Ignorant** means not having learned.
*They tend to assume that people in earlier times were **ignorant.***

**Stupid** means not able to learn.
*Just because he's uninformed, does not necessarily mean he's **stupid.***

## Illegible, unreadable

**Illegible** means the handwriting is impossible to read.
*For me, not the pharmacist, the prescription is **illegible.***

**Unreadable** means the material is uninteresting or badly worded.
*The grammatical errors made the letter simply **unreadable.***

## Illicit, elicit

*See entry for **Elicit, illicit.***

## Illusion, delusion, allusion

*See entry for **Allusion, delusion, illusion.***

## Illusive, elusive

*See entry for **Elusive, illusive.***

## Imaginary, imaginative

**Imaginary** means not real but just imagined.
***Imaginary** friends are typical for children between the ages of 3 and 6.*

**Imaginative** means to show an imagination.
*Jim Henson's **imaginative** ability brought much joy to many families.*

## Immanent, imminent, eminent

*See entry for **Eminent, immanent, imminent.***

## Immature, premature

**Immature** means not developed, not full grown, or not completed.
*That child appears **immature** compared with the rest of the class.*

**Premature** means before the expected time, not ready, or too soon.
*The task group's findings on the investigation are **premature.***

## Immerge, immerse, emerge

*See entry for* ***Emerge, immerge, immerse.***

## Immigrant, emigrant, migrant

*See entry for* ***Emigrant, immigrant, migrant.***

## Immoral, amoral

*See entry for* ***Amoral, immoral.***

## Immunity, impunity

**Immunity** means exempt from disease or obligation.
*The new vaccine provides* ***immunity*** *against the disease.*
*The state agency was granted* ***immunity*** *from any local taxation.*

**Impunity** means exempt from harm, penalty, or punishment.
*A key witness was guaranteed* ***impunity*** *in exchange for his testimony.*

## Impassable, impassible

**Impassable** means not passable or cannot be traveled over.
*This road is* ***impassable*** *not only in winter but in early spring as well.*

**Impassible**, a theological term, means incapable of suffering.
*Some believe that God does not suffer and is therefore* ***impassible.***

## Impel, induce

**Impel** means to urge or force an action.
*The factories are **impelled** to follow the new environmental regulations.*

**Induce** means to persuade or to cause to do something.
*The exceptional video quality **induced** us to buy a DVD player.*
*The doctor prescribed a mild drug to **induce** sleep.*

## Implicit, explicit

*See entry for **Explicit, implicit**.*

## Imply, infer

**Imply** means to convey or suggest a meaning indirectly.
*Jack's memo **implies** that the project would be delayed another week.*

**Infer** means to conclude from facts or premises.
*She **infers** from the evidence that the accused is not guilty.*

Memory hook: Speakers and writers **imply**; listeners and readers **infer**.

## Impostor, imposture

An **impostor** is a person who pretends to be someone else.
*The **impostor** felt he could bluff his way through every checkpoint.*

**Imposture** is the act of deception.
*Laws exist against the **imposture** of hyping worthless stocks.*

## Impracticable, impractical

**Impracticable** means impossible of being done or put into practice.
*The extensive damage made reassembling the aircraft **impracticable.***

**Impractical** means a course of action with little practical value.
*A plan for a new city venue would probably be seen as **impractical.***

## Impulsive, compulsive

*See entry for **Compulsive, compulsory, impulsive.***

## In depth, indepth

**In depth** is always two words.
*Let us take an **in depth** look at news stories from around the world.*

## In fact, infact

**In fact** is always two words.
***In fact**, it is a surprise that we score as well as we do.*

## In regard to, in regards to

**In regard to**, without an *s*, is the correct phrase. Sometimes you can avoid this phrase by substituting words like *on*, *about*, or *concerning*.
*She notified everyone **in regard to** (on, about, concerning) the time change.*

## Inalienable, unalienable

Either word is correct, but **inalienable** is more common today.

## Incidentally, incidently

**Incidentally** means by chance or not intentionally.
***Incidentally**, you have a writing style that many readers like.*

Incidently is not a word.

## Incite, insight

**Incite** means to arouse or provoke action.
*Some political views tend to promote or **incite** debate within the party.*

**Insight** refers to mental vision or understanding.
*Harold is offering his own **insights** on how to invest carefully online.*

## Inclose, enclose

**Enclose** is preferred in American usage.
*Please ensure you **enclose** your latest resume with the job application.*

## Incredible, incredulous

**Incredible** means hard to believe or unbelievable.
*Ed's quick explanation of the car accident is simply **incredible.***

**Incredulous** means not believing or skeptical.
*Rob's story of flying saucers received a few **incredulous** stares.*

## Indeterminable, indeterminate

**Indeterminable** means impossible to find out, fix, measure, or decide.
*The impact on the number of permit applications is **indeterminable**.*

**Indeterminate** means vague or unclear.
*Spatial objects with **indeterminate** boundaries are difficult to model.*

## Indict, indite

**Indict** means to accuse or formally charge.
*Do you know if the grand jury is going to **indict** the suspect this week?*

**Indite** means to compose or put into writing.
*The former president seldom uses a writer to help **indite** his speeches.*

## Indictment, arraignment

*See entry for **Arraignment, indictment**.*

## Indifferent, ambiguous, ambivalent

*See entry for **Ambiguous, ambivalent, indifferent**.*

## Indigenous, indigent, indignant

**Indigenous** means native.
***Indigenous** cultures have contributed to several medical discoveries.*

**Indigent** means in need of money, impoverished, or poor.
*The state and local government provide medical care for **indigent** families.*

**Indignant** means angry.
*A full and detailed explanation backs Phil's **indignant** denial.*

## Inductive, deductive

*See entry for* ***Deductive, inductive.***

## Inequity, iniquity

**Inequity** refers to injustice or unfairness.
*Many voters are unhappy about the **inequity** of the new voting system.*

**Iniquity** refers to immorality, sin, or wickedness.
*Justin sought to investigate the **iniquity** done by the other group.*

## Inexplicable, inextricable

**Inexplicable** means difficult or impossible to account for.
*The TV show's **inexplicable** popularity is keeping the sponsors happy.*

**Inextricable** means difficult or impossible to avoid.
*The meeting conflict is **inextricably** linked to our lack of communication.*

## Infamous, famous, notorious

*See entry for* ***Famous, infamous, notorious.***

## Infectious, contagious

*See entry for* ***Contagious, infectious.***

## Inflammable, flammable, nonflammable

*See entry for **Flammable, inflammable, nonflammable.***

## Inflict, afflict

*See entry for **Afflict, inflict.***

## Ingenious, ingenuous, disingenuous

*See entry for **Disingenuous, ingenious, ingenuous.***

## Innumerable, endless

*See entry for **Endless, innumerable.***

## Inquire, enquire

**Inquire** is the preferred spelling, but either one is acceptable.

## Insidious, invidious

**Insidious** means spreading harm in a subtle way.
*Her constant criticism has an **insidious** effect on the team's morale.*

**Invidious** means being discriminatory or causing resentment.
*The new laws appear to be unjust and **invidious.***

## Insoluble, insolvable, insolvent

**Insoluble** means incapable of being dissolved.
*The high-protein soy powder is **insoluble** in milk.*

**Insolvable** means it cannot be solved.
*The corporation continues to have **insolvable** quality problems.*

**Insolvent** means incapable of paying debts.
*The new owners are selling many assets of those **insolvent** companies.*

## Install, instill

**Install** means to put into position or to set up.
*Katie is going to **install** the new software after work.*

**Instill** means to implant or introduce gradually.
*The short preparation is not enough time to **instill** confidence.*

## Instinct, intuition

**Instinct** is a behavior, a tendency, or an aptitude born in an individual.
*A bear's **instinct** makes the animal hibernate in the winter.*

**Intuition** is knowledge learned through personal experiences.
*Joanne's **intuition** told her to leave the stock market before it crashed.*

## Insure, assure, ensure

*See entry for **Assure, ensure, insure.***

## Intense, intensive

**Intense** means occurring in an extreme degree or powerful.
*The heat last summer was so **intense**, people remained mainly indoors.*

**Intensive** means concentrated or thorough.
*Our region of the state was subjected to **intensive** heat all last summer.*

## Intentionally, advisedly

*See entry for **Advisedly, intentionally**.*

## Interpolate, extrapolate

*See entry for **Extrapolate, interpolate**.*

## Interpret, interpretate

**Interpretate** is not a word.

## Interstate, intestate, intrastate

**Interstate** means between states.
*The **interstate** long distance rate drops on the weekends.*

**Intestate** means without making a will.
*The law of **intestate** succession can vary from state to state.*

**Intrastate** means within one state.
*The bill attempts to specifically regulate **intrastate** commerce.*

## Intrust, entrust

**Entrust** is preferred in American usage.
*They **entrust** our team with the management of their financial affairs.*

## Inure, enure

**Inure**, meaning to get used to something undesirable, is the preferred word.
*Considering where we live, we are **inured** to frequent power outages.*

## Invent, discover

*See entry for **Discover, invent.***

## Invigorate, enervate

*See entry for **Enervate, invigorate.***

## Invoke, evince, evoke

*See entry for **Evince, evoke, invoke.***

## Inward, inwards

**Inward** is preferred in American usage.

## IP protocol

Redundancy. **IP** means *Internet Protocol.* Just use **IP**.

## IPO offering

Redundancy. **IPO** means *Initial Program Offering*. Just use **IPO.**

## IRA account

Redundancy. **IRA** means *Individual Retirement Account*. Just use **IRA.**

## Irascible, erasable

*See entry for* ***Erasable, irascible.***

## Irregardless, regardless

**Irregardless** is a nonstandard word. Avoid its use.

**Regardless** means without regard or unmindful.
*The foursome plays every Saturday* ***regardless*** *of the weather.*

## Irrelevant, irreverent

**Irrelevant** means not pertinent or not relating to the subject.
*Some of the testimony in the case seemed like* ***irrelevant*** *information.*

**Irreverent** means disrespectful, satirical, or lacking reverence.
*A few critics took an* ***irreverent*** *look at the lesser-known film.*

## Irritate, aggravate

*See entry for* ***Aggravate, irritate.***

## Irruption, eruption

*See entry for* ***Eruption, irruption.***

## ISBN number

Redundancy. **ISBN** means *International Standard Book Number*. Just use **ISBN**.

## ISDN network

Redundancy. **ISDN** means *Integrated Services Digital Network*. Just use **ISDN**.

## Isle, aisle

*See entry for* ***Aisle, isle.***

## ISP provider

Redundancy. **ISP** means *Internet Service Provider*. Just use **ISP**.

## Its, it's

**Its** is a possessive pronoun that is never split by an apostrophe.
*Though old and outdated, our first computer has served* ***its*** *purpose.*

**It's** is the contracted or shortened form of *it is*.
***It's*** *definitely much faster than our first computer.*

Memory hook: Possessive **its** never splits.

# J

*"The most valuable of all talents is that of never using two words when one will do."* — Thomas Jefferson

## Jest, gist

*See entry for **Gist, jest.***

## Jetsam, flotsam

*See entry for **Flotsam, jetsam.***

## Jibe, gibe

*See entry for **Gibe, jibe.***

## Judgement, judgment

**Judgment** without the *e* is preferred in American usage.
*We reserve **judgment** until all the facts are available.*

## Judicial, judicious, juridical

**Judicial** refers to the law courts or judges.
*The **Judicial** Branch is one of the three branches of the U.S. Government.*

**Judicious** refers to a person's careful or wise judgment.
*Many taxpayers would like to see more examples of **judicious** spending.*

**Juridical** refers to the administration of justice.
*He proceeded to fulfill the **juridical** requirements related to that case.*

# K

*"Words are, of course, the most powerful drug used by mankind."* — Rudyard Kipling

## Karat, carat, caret, carrot

*See entry for* ***Carat, caret, carrot, karat.***

## Kind of, sort of

Avoid these awkward phrases if you mean ***somewhat.***
*Last night's concert was* ***somewhat*** *(not* ***kind of*** *or* ***sort of****) disappointing.*

## Koala bear

A **koala** is a marsupial not a bear. Just call these little animals **koalas.**

# L

*"So difficult is it to show the various meanings and imperfections of words when we have nothing else but words to do it with."* — John Locke

## Lapse, elapse

*See entry for* ***Elapse, lapse.***

## Latter, former

*See entry for* ***Former, latter.***

## Lawful, legal

**Lawful** means rightful or in accordance with the law.
*The elder son is the* ***lawful*** *heir to much of the estate.*
*Transfer the ownership of the house and property in a* ***lawful*** *way.*

**Legal** means relating to the law.
*The* ***legal*** *authorities are addressing the downloading of Internet music.*

## Lay, lie

**Lay** means to place or to put something; it requires a direct object.
*Where are you going to* ***lay*** *that egg?*
*I am* ***laying*** *the egg on the kitchen counter.*
*He* ***laid*** *the egg on the kitchen counter.*

**Lie** means to be in a horizontal position; it never takes an object.
*The baseball* ***lies*** *in the street next to the car.*
*The baseball is* ***lying*** *by the car.*
*How long has the baseball* ***lain*** *in the street?*

## LCD display

Redundancy. **LCD** means *Liquid Crystal Display*. Just use **LCD**.

## Leak, leek

**Leak** refers to the escape or passage of something.
*Once they discovered the news* ***leak****, they called a press conference.*

**Leek** refers to an edible plant (part of the onion family).
*Rick's garden last summer contained beets, tomatoes, and* ***leeks****.*

## Lean, lien

**Lean** means free of fat or to incline.
*Venison is* ***lean*** *compared with many meats we have eaten.*
*Do not* ***lean*** *against that side of the wall for fear you may get hurt.*

**Lien** means a legal claim to something.
*The bank has a* ***lien*** *against their vacation home in New Jersey.*

## Learn, teach

**Learn** means to acquire information or knowledge.
*This computer game allows people to* ***learn*** *how to read music quickly.*

**Teach** means to impart knowledge or information.
*Some English teachers still* ***teach*** *how to diagram sentences.*

## Leave, let

**Leave** means to allow to remain or to go away.
*If you* ***leave*** *the book with me, I'll be sure to read it.*
*If you* ***leave*** *quietly, no one in the library will be disturbed.*

**Let** means to allow or to permit.
*Please* ***let*** *me help you with your chemistry homework.*

Note: When **leave** or **let** is used with the word *alone*, these words are interchangeable.
***Leave*** *(****let****) Gerry alone while he is doing his homework.*

## Lectern, podium

**Lectern** is a small stand that supports papers or books.
**Podium** is an elevated platform where one stands.

Memory hook: You stand behind a *lectern* and on a *podium*.

## LED diode

Redundancy. LED means *Light Emitting Diode*. Just use LED.

## Legislator, legislature

**Legislator** refers to a lawmaker.
*Our* ***legislator*** *proposes a law that limits the sale of tobacco products.*

**Legislature** refers to a group of lawmakers.
*This year's election brought 10 new members to the county* ***legislature.***

## Lend, loan

**Lend** is a verb.
*Please* ***lend*** *me 20 dollars.*

**Loan** is a noun.
*The 20 dollars is a gift not a* ***loan.***

Note: Although careful writers maintain this distinction, it is common to see **lend** and **loan** used interchangeably as verbs.

## Less, fewer

*See entry for* **Fewer, less, lest.**

## Lessee, lessor

**Lessee** refers to a lease holder or tenant.
*The* ***lessee*** *makes the rental payments on the 15th of every month.*

**Lessor** refers to a lease grantor or landlord.
*The* ***lessor*** *keeps full ownership rights of the apartment.*

## Lessen, lesson

**Lessen** means to diminish or become less.
*His broker believes that money market funds may* ***lessen*** *investment risk.*

**Lesson** means something to be learned.
*The new software helps teachers make clear and detailed* ***lesson*** *plans.*

## Let's us

Redundancy. **Let's** is a contraction for *let us.* Just use **let's.**

## Levee, levy

**Levee** is a formal reception or an embankment.
*The new leader was introduced that evening at a* ***levee*** *near the embassy.*
*After the* ***levee*** *broke, the town quickly evacuated.*

**Levy,** a verb, means to collect, to enlist in military service, or to begin war.
*The court could* ***levy*** *a fine for misappropriating the funds.*
*They are going to* ***levy*** *troops from the countryside.*
*They want to avoid* ***levying*** *war at all costs.*

**Levy,** a noun, is a charge imposed or the act of levying money, property, or troops.
*The tax rate* ***levy*** *is a real challenge this year.*
*The recent* ***levy*** *raised few troops for the military.*

## Liable, libel, lible, slander

**Liable** means legally responsible or a good chance.
*The jury quickly found him* ***liable*** *for fraud and other things.*
*Considering the dark clouds, it is* ***liable*** *to rain today.*

**Libel** means damaging someone's reputation in print or other media.
*The inaccurate story prompted him to sue the magazine for **libel.***

**Lible** is not a word.

**Slander** is an oral statement intended to damage a person's reputation.
*His negative comments toward him were definitely taken as **slander.***

## Lightening, lightning

**Lightening** means making lighter.
*John can never be accused of **lightening** the load on hospitality.*

**Lightning** refers to thunder and lightning.
*If you are not careful, golf clubs can act like **lightning** rods.*

## Like, as

*See entry for **As, like.***

## Likely, apt

*See entry for **Apt, likely.***

## Limit, limitation

**Limit** refers to a physical or political boundary.
*Researchers feel there may be no **limit** to how long people can live.*

**Limitation** refers to a restraint or restriction.
*Some states have a **limitation** on cell phone use in cars.*

## Litany, liturgy

**Litany** refers to a form of prayer or a lengthy list.
*The **Litany** of the Saints is read at our church every Sunday.*
*The accused faced a **litany** of questions about his whereabouts last night.*

**Liturgy** refers to the prescribed form for a public religious service.
*Today's worship service is built around the **liturgy** of celebration.*

## Literally, figuratively

*See entry for **Figuratively, literally**.*

## Loath, loathe

**Loath** means reluctant or unwilling.
*Henry is **loath** to move despite the attractive job offer.*

**Loathe** means to dislike intensely.
*Every month we **loathe** receiving those credit card bills.*

## Locale, locality, location

**Locale** is a place that refers to a particular event or occurrence.
*The film producers found an ideal **locale** in Mexico for the sequel.*

**Locality** is a particular neighborhood, place, or district.
*Our vacation house is in a quiet **locality** not too far from the shore.*

**Location** is a place where something is situated.
*The new course is built on a mountaintop **location** just outside the city.*

## Loose, lose

**Loose** means unrestrained or not tight.
*Giant icebergs continue to shake* ***loose*** *off the Antarctic coast.*

**Lose** means to mislay or miss out on something.
*By not accepting credit cards, companies can* ***lose*** *potential sales.*

## Luxuriant, luxurious

**Luxuriant** refers to something abundant, profuse, or rich.
***Luxuriant*** *lawns and gardens surround the hotel on all sides.*

**Luxurious** refers to luxury.
*The vacation package includes a weekend stay at a* ***luxurious*** *hotel.*

# M

*"I love writing. I love the swirl and swing of words as they tangle with human emotions."* — James A. Michener

## Magnate, magnet

**Magnate** is an influential or powerful person (usually in business).
*Each year the shipping **magnate** donates money to cancer research.*

**Magnet** is a person or thing that exerts attraction.
*The low cost of living there could become a **magnet** for the retired.*

## Magnificent, magniloquent, munificent

**Magnificent** means grand or splendid.
*San Simeon's Hearst Castle has a **magnificent** view of the Pacific Ocean.*

**Magniloquent** means colorful, extravagant, or lofty in speech.
*I find the professor's **magniloquent** talks entertaining but also confusing.*

**Munificent** means extremely generous.
*The celebrities gave a **munificent** donation to the relief effort.*

## Majority, plurality

**Majority** means more than 50 percent.
*The **majority** of the country favored last year's tax cut.*

**Plurality** means the most of something, regardless of percentage.
*In 1992, Clinton won the Presidency with a **plurality** of the votes cast.*

## Mantel, mantle

A **mantel** is a shelf (mantelpiece).
*Mary and Doug placed a prized piece of art over their fireplace **mantel.***

A **mantle** is a cloak or something that covers like a cloak.
*This morning a **mantle** of fog hung over the valley for a few hours.*

## Many, much

**Many** refers to countable items or units.
***Many** of our car troubles disappeared by using a higher octane fuel.*

**Much** refers to noncountable items or units.
*Low octane fuel caused **much** of our car trouble.*

## Marked, remarkable

**Marked** means clearly defined and evident.
*We noticed that Jack has a **marked** limp when he walks.*

**Remarkable** means extraordinary or worthy of notice.
*We noticed a **remarkable** improvement in Gerry's grades.*

## Masterful, masterly

**Masterful** means domineering or powerful.
*General George Patton was a **masterful** soldier and leader.*

**Masterly** means highly skilled or the knowledge of a master.
*His spring concert was a* ***masterly*** *performance of Bach.*

## Material, materiel

**Material** is the substance from which something is composed.
*His new suit is made of a light blue silk* ***material.***

**Materiel** is the equipment or supplies used by an organization.
*We have one department in our military company for just* ***materiel.***

## May, can

*See entry for* ***Can, may.***

## May be, maybe

**May be** is a verb phrase indicating possibility.
*It* ***may be*** *necessary to ask for an outside specialist or a second opinion.*

**Maybe** is an adverb meaning perhaps.
***Maybe*** *the legal staff can resolve this issue within a few days.*

## May have, may of

**May have** is the correct phrase.
*As you* ***may have*** *heard by now, tonight's class has been cancelled.*

## Mean, median

**Mean**, a noun, is the center point between two extremes.
*The arithmetic* ***mean*** *of 1, 2, 3 is 2.*

**Median**, a noun, is a center value, road barrier, or line within a triangle.
*The* ***median*** *salary for engineers is lower than you think.*
*The concrete* ***median*** *divided the six-lane freeway in Los Angeles.*
*The centroid is where the three* ***medians*** *of a triangle intersect.*

## Mean, mien

**Mean**, an adjective, means lacking kindness or potentially harmful.
*Though the dog looks* ***mean,*** *he is just a playful puppy.*

**Mien**, a noun, refers to a person's manner or appearance.
*Annie is known for her noble* ***mien,*** *virtue, and great appeal.*

## Meantime, meanwhile

Both words refer to an intervening time.

**Meantime** is commonly used as a noun.
*In the* ***meantime,*** *we continue to wait for another opportunity.*

**Meanwhile** is commonly used as an adverb.
***Meanwhile,*** *we waited an extra hour for the children to arrive.*

## Meddle, mettle

**Meddle** means to interfere with something.
*We have no desire to* ***meddle*** *in the local politics of our community.*

**Mettle** refers to the quality or strength of a person's character.
*Rachel is being given a chance to prove her* ***mettle*** *and worth.*

## Media are, media is

**Media are** is the correct phrase because **media** is the plural of *medium.*
*All the news **media are** covering the events of the trial.*

## Mediate, arbitrate

*See entry for **Adjudicate, arbitrate, mediate.***

## Memento, momento

**Memento** is a special remembrance or souvenir.
*Joe brought back a beautiful **memento** from England to give to his wife.*

Note: In the Catholic Church, **memento** refers to the Canon of the Mass.

**Momento** is not a word.

## Meritorious, meritous

The correct word is **meritorious.**
*They are being recognized for their **meritorious** service to the team.*

## Meteorology, metrology

**Meteorology** is the science of weather. **Metrology** is the science of measurement.

## Method, methodology

**Method** is a way in which to do something.
*What **method** did the golf pro use to fix Bill's slice?*

**Methodology** is a set of methods, practices, procedures, or rules.
*Dan introduced a different **methodology** from which to do linguistics.*

## Meticulous, scrupulous

**Meticulous** means exact, finicky, or precise.
*The Binghamton artist shows a **meticulous** attention to detail.*

**Scrupulous** means conscientious or principled.
*A **scrupulous** character usually tries to stay within the letter of the law.*

## Might have, might of

**Might have** is the correct phrase.
*Do you think they **might have** a problem with the new regulations?*

## Militate, mitigate

**Militate** means to act against, influence adversely, or oppose.
*The leader's anger **militated** against any hope of a truce.*

**Mitigate** means to diminish in severity or lessen.
*The physical therapy for my neck **mitigated** the severe pain.*

## Millenary, millinery

**Millenary** refers to a total of 1,000. **Millinery** refers to women's hats.

## Minimize, diminish

*See entry for **Diminish, minimize.***

## Miniscule, minuscule

Preferred spelling is **minuscule**.
*The comprehensive study shows the disadvantages are **minuscule** at best.*

## Mishap, accident, incident

*See entry for **Accident, incident, mishap.***

## Misinformation, disinformation

*See entry for **Disinformation, misinformation.***

## Misplace, displace

*See entry for **Displace, misplace.***

## Moot point, mute point

**Moot point** is the correct phrase. The phrase originally meant *open to debate*, but now it can also mean *not worth debating*.
*Whether the person deserves the award is a **moot point**.*

## Moral, morale

**Moral** refers to a lesson from a story or being righteous or ethical.
*What **moral** or message can be drawn from today's reading?*
*They continually show a **moral** dimension to their actions.*

**Morale** refers to the spirit or state of mind.
*Despite the surprise loss, we maintain a high team **morale**.*

## More important, more importantly

Either phrase is acceptable, though some purists prefer **more important**.
***More important** (**importantly**), we will generate more interest in reading.*

## More than, over

**More than** refers to countable items.
***More than** 500 churches are in upstate New York.*

**Over** refers to general amounts or unspecified increments.
***Over** half of the inventory is unsold, resulting in a huge loss.*

## Most, almost

*See entry for **Almost, most**.*

## Mother-in-laws, mothers-in-law

**Mothers-in-law** is the correct phrase.

## MST time

Redundancy. **MST** means *Mountain Standard Time.* Just use **MST**.

## Muchly

**Muchly** is not a word.
*We would **much** (not **muchly**) appreciate your attendance tonight.*

## Multilateral, bilateral, unilateral

*See entry for **Bilateral, multilateral, unilateral.***

## Must have, must of

**Must have** is the correct phrase.
*The bank **must have** seen that foreclosure coming for weeks.*

## Mutual, common

*See entry for **Common, mutual, ordinary, popular.***

## Mysterious, mystical

**Mysterious** means beyond human comprehension or unintelligible.
*A **mysterious** craft appeared in the sky and left us all wondering.*

**Mystical** means hidden from human knowledge (spiritual).
*The Blessed Mother's appearance at Fatima is a **mystical** experience.*

# N

*"Those for whom words have lost their value are likely to find that ideas have also lost their value."* — Edwin Newman

## NAFTA agreement

Redundancy. **NAFTA** means *North American Free Trade Agreement*. Just use **NAFTA**.

## NATO organization

Redundancy. **NATO** means *North Atlantic Treaty Organization*. Just use **NATO**.

## Nauseated, nauseous

**Nauseated** means to feel sick.
*Joe feels **nauseated** 20 minutes after his workout.*

**Nauseous** means something sickening.
*The neighbors refuse to put up with that **nauseous** stench.*

## Neither, either

*See entry for **Either, neither**.*

## NIC card

Redundancy. **NIC** means *Network Interface Card*. Just use **NIC**.

## No body, nobody

**No body** means no group.
***No body*** *of rules enacted by them can be called perfect.*

**Nobody** means no person.
*Star Trek went where* ***nobody*** *had gone before.*

## No one

Always spell this as two words.
***No one*** *picks up the mail while we are away.*

## No sooner than, no sooner when

**No sooner than** is the correct phrase. In this phrase, the word **sooner** is a comparative adverb and should be followed by the word **than** (not **when**).
*We had* ***no sooner*** *left the game* ***than*** *the next batter hit a home run.*

## Nohow

**Nohow,** nonstandard for *in no way* or *not at all*, should be avoided.
*The clerk could* ***in no way*** (not **nohow**) *decipher his handwriting.*

## Noisome, noisy

**Noisome** means foul-smelling, noxious, or offensive.
*The* ***noisome*** *odor coming from the river bothers many residents.*

**Noisy** means making much noise.
*Despite the PC's high price, the keyboard is quite* ***noisy.***

## Northward, northwards

**Northward** is preferred in American usage.

## Notable, noticeable

**Notable** means worthy of notice.
*Her accomplishments in both software and hardware are* ***notable.***

**Noticeable** means readily observed.
*The construction crew is making* ***noticeable*** *progress on the building.*

## Novice, amateur

*See entry for* ***Amateur, novice.***

## Nowheres

Always use **nowhere.**

## NPR radio

Redundancy. **NPR** means *National Public Radio*. Just use **NPR.**

## Number, amount

*See entry for* ***Amount, number.***

## Numerable, numerous

**Numerable** means something that can be counted or numbered.
*If the data is not **numerable**, the impact cannot be measured.*

**Numerous** means a great number of or many.
*The election officials made an effort to save **numerous** flawed ballots.*

# O

*"Language ought to be the joint creation of poets and manual workers."* — George Orwell

## Oblivious, obvious

**Oblivious** means unmindful of something.
*For a time, I was **oblivious** to the danger of the sun's ultra violet rays.*

**Obvious** means easily perceived or understood.
*Our services present unique and **obvious** benefits for your company.*

## Observance, observation

**Observance** refers to the following of a custom, duty, or law.
*The **observance** of Veterans Day varies from one organization to another.*

**Observation** refers to the act of noticing or recording something.
*The lab technician made careful **observations** during the experiment.*

## Obtain, attain

*See entry for **Attain, obtain.***

## Obtuse, abstruse

*See entry for **Abstruse, obtuse.***

## Occultist, oculist

**Occultist** is one who believes in dark forces, witchcraft, and other supernatural things.
*An **occultist** would usually reject astronomy in favor of astrology.*

**Oculist** is a physician who treats eyes (synonymous with ophthalmologist and optometrist).
***Oculist** Dr. Zhivago identified the elements that contribute to sight.*

## Official, officious

**Official** means authorized, formal, or of an office.
*Here is an **official** announcement: the dance floor is now open.*
*The **official** always makes the final ruling.*

**Officious** means eager to offer advice or service when not requested.
*People usually fight any **officious** interference with their liberties.*

## Often, oftentimes

**Often** is the preferred and simpler word to use.
***Often*** (not ***oftentimes***) *we exercise immediately after work.*

## Old-fashion, old-fashioned

**Old-fashioned,** meaning outdated, is the correct phrase to use.
*Bob uses an **old-fashioned** approach for teaching applied math.*

## Omnipresent, omniscient

**Omnipresent** means to be present everywhere simultaneously.
*Technological change is **omnipresent** throughout the world.*

**Omniscient** means to be all knowing or have total knowledge.
*If they were **omniscient**, they would know something no one else knows.*

## Omnivorous, carnivorous, herbivorous

*See entry for **Carnivorous, herbivorous, omnivorous.***

## On route, en route

*See entry for **En route, on route.***

## On to, onto

**On to** is used when **on** is an adverb and **to** is a preposition.
*The engineers then moved **on to** the next phase of the project.*

**Onto** means to move to a position or to be aware of something.
*You can transfer pictures **onto** your computer in a few steps.*
*We are **onto** your plan for restructuring the company.*

## One and the same, one in the same

**One and the same** is the correct phrase.
*To some people, asteroids and comets are **one and the same.***

## One another, each other

*See entry for* ***Each other, one another.***

## One of the best, one of the only

Avoid these phrases. Because each phrase refers to just one thing, they are seen as contradictions. **One of the few** is a better choice.
*California is* ***one of the few*** *states we visited last year on our vacation.*

## Onward, onwards

**Onward** is preferred in American usage.

## Opaque, translucent, transparent

**Opaque** means not permitting light to pass through or reflect.
*Oil paints are usually* ***opaque*** *and traditionally used on canvas.*

**Translucent** means permitting light to pass through without clarity.
***Translucent*** *bond paper provides good line quality and little ink bleed.*

**Transparent** means permitting light to pass through with clarity.
*Glass, although* ***transparent*** *to visible light, absorbs infrared rays.*

## OPEC countries

Redundancy. **OPEC** means *Organization of the Petroleum Exporting Countries.* Just use **OPEC.**

## Ophthalmologist, optician, optometrist

**Ophthalmologist** - an M.D., specializes in treating eye diseases.
**Optician** - makes and sells glasses and other optical equipment.
**Optometrist** - examines one's vision and prescribes corrective glasses.

## Oppose, appose

*See entry for **Appose, oppose.***

## Opposite, apposite

*See entry for **Apposite, opposite.***

## Oral, aural

*See entry for **Aural, oral.***

## Oral, verbal

**Oral** and **verbal** both refer to things spoken; however, only **verbal** refers to things written.
*Graduate students are required to do three **oral** reports this semester.*
*Writer Albert M. Joseph has a **verbal** mastery of our language.*

## Ordinal numbers, cardinal numbers

*See entry for **Cardinal numbers, ordinal numbers.***

## Ordinance, ordnance

**Ordinance** refers to a decree, law, or regulation.
*An* ***ordinance*** *to improve the city's parks is on the table for discussion.*

**Ordnance** refers to military equipment or weapons.
*The new technology can help locate unexploded* ***ordnance*** *and mines.*

## Ordinary, common, mutual, popular

*See entry for* ***Common, mutual, ordinary, popular.***

## Orient, orientate

Preferred word is **orient.**
*Fortunately, we have plenty of time to* ***orient*** *ourselves with the project.*

## Ostensibly, ostentatiously

**Ostensibly** means apparently, evidently, or presumably.
*It's a story* ***ostensibly*** *for kids, but even more appreciated by adults.*

**Ostentatiously** means flaunting or pretentious.
*They rarely dress* ***ostentatiously*** *and never flaunt their wealth.*

## Out loud, aloud

*See entry for* ***Aloud, out loud.***

## Outmost, utmost

**Outmost** means outermost or farthest out.
*Janet and Jim made a trip to the **outmost** reaches of northern Alaska.*

**Utmost** usually means greatest amount, degree, or intensity.
*Our department treats all information with **utmost** confidentiality.*

## Outward, outwards

**Outward** is preferred in American usage.

## Over, more than

*See entry for **More than, over.***

## Overt, covert

*See entry for **Covert, overt.***

## Overweening, overwhelming

**Overweening** means conceited, overbearing, or pretentious.
*We pondered if his **overweening** ego would fit with the rest of the team.*

**Overwhelming** means overpowering in effect or strength.
*Doctors feel the artificial heart is an **overwhelming** medical success.*

# P

*"A good word makes the heart glad."* — Proverbs

## Palate, palette, pallet

**Palate** is the roof of your mouth that gives the sense of taste.
*A common defect in the roof of the mouth is called a cleft **palate.***

**Palette** is a hand-held board that an artists uses for mixing paint.
*His brush and **palette** captures the beauty of the Adirondack Mountains.*

**Pallet** is a flat platform where goods are loaded.
*Several **pallets** at the warehouse contain new DVD players.*

## Parameter, perimeter

**Parameter** is a quantity or mathematical variable that stays constant.
*The applet can be customized by using the **parameters** in the HTML file.*

**Perimeter** is something that has a boundary or a limit.
*When no one is home, the dog does not leave the **perimeter** of the yard.*

## Paramount, tantamount

**Paramount** means the main concern or chief importance.
*Customer satisfaction is a **paramount** concern to our sales team.*

**Tantamount** means the same as or equivalent.
*The general's action is **tantamount** to a declaration of peace.*

## Partially, partly

**Partially** means to a certain degree or extent.
*The company **partially** shut down for 2 weeks to save energy.*

**Partly** means being in some part or not completely.
*Scientists believe infections may be **partly** responsible for mental illness.*

## Passable, passible

**Passable** means barely satisfactory or able to be passed.
*We sat through just a **passable** performance of "Hamlet" last night.*
*Whether the roads are **passable** depends on the weather conditions.*

**Passible**, a theological term, means capable of feeling or suffering.
*Some theologians believe that God does suffer and is therefore **passible**.*

## Passed, past

**Passed** refers to the action of passing.
*Both the House and Senate **passed** electronic signature bills last year.*

**Past** refers to time or distance.
*The documentary is about computer history, from the **past** to the present.*

## Passport, visa

**Passport** is an official government document that certifies a person's identity and citizenship and permits travel to another country. **Visa** is an official authorization stamped to a passport that permits a person's entry into and travel within a country.

## Patience, patients

**Patience** refers to the ability to wait.
*__Patience__ is a virtue we should all practice.*

**Patients** refers to people under medical treatment.
*Most __patients__ can expect some relief within 2 to 4 days.*

## PDF format

Redundancy. **PDF** means *Portable Document Format*. Just use PDF.

## Peaceable, peaceful

**Peaceable** means inclined to peace.
*The two companies met in a __peaceable__ spirit to resolve the differences.*

**Peaceful** means tranquil or a state of peace or calm.
*We are committed to making a safe and __peaceful__ environment.*

## Peak, peek, pique

**Peak**, as a noun, means the summit; as a verb, it means to maximize.
*With those record times, Gracie is at the __peak__ of her running career.*
*At what age did you __peak__ in your running career?*

**Peek** means to peep or snoop.
*__Peek__ into the window to see if Karol and Jo have left the house.*

**Pique** means to excite or irritate.
*Did you **pique** someone's curiosity and interest?*
*After hearing those comments, Ed is definitely **piqued**.*

## Penultimate, ultimate

**Penultimate** means next to last.
*Next week is the **penultimate** week of the fall semester.*

**Ultimate** means last or quite superlative.
*The collision and **ultimate** fate of Titanic occurred on April 14, 1912.*
*Mary prepared the **ultimate** apple pie for my birthday.*

## Percent, percentage

**Percent** is specific and is usually used with a number.
*They expect to reduce their workforce by an additional 15 **percent**.*

**Percentage** is not specific and is never used with a number.
*The workforce reduction affects a small **percentage** of engineering.*

Note: **Percent** should be spelled as one word and not two (**per cent**). Also, **percent** is becoming more accepted without a number by it.
*What **percent** of your workday is spent in meetings?*

## Perfume, cologne

*See entry for **Cologne, perfume**.*

## Periodic, sporadic

**Periodic** means occurring at regular or predictable intervals.
*Lisa told us she would be having **periodic** performance reviews.*

**Sporadic** means occurring at irregular or unpredictable times.
*Some western states are experiencing **sporadic** shortages of power.*

## Perpetrate, perpetuate

**Perpetrate** means being responsible for something.
*Bill likes to **perpetrate** a few practical jokes on his teammates.*

**Perpetuate** means to cause to be remembered or last indefinitely.
*The Vietnam Memorial **perpetuates** the memory of many veterans.*

## Perquisite, prerequisite

**Perquisite** refers to a special benefit or privilege (a **perq**).
*A new company car is a **perquisite** for all their executives.*

**Prerequisite** refers to something required in advance.
*What **prerequisite** course does the college require for admission?*

## Persecute, prosecute

**Persecute** means to harass or treat unjustly.
*In the U.S., it is unlawful to **persecute** people for their religious beliefs.*

**Prosecute** means to enforce by legal action.
*Some states **prosecute** juveniles as adults in criminal court.*

## Person that, person who

**Person who** is the preferred phrase in formal writing and speaking. Some purists reserve **who** for people and **that** for animals or things.

*Jeff is the person* ***who*** *chose engineering as a career.*
*That's the elephant* ***that*** *lost its memory.*

## Personal, personnel

**Personal** means private.
*The supervisor did not want to discuss any* ***personal*** *matters at work.*

**Personnel** means the Human Resources area or a group of people.
*The* ***Personnel*** *Department handles the employee's exit interview.*
*We have the qualified* ***personnel*** *to get the job done.*

## Perspective, prospective

**Perspective** is a point of view or a method for creating the illusion of depth.
*From the art teacher's* ***perspective****, it provides another way of learning.*
*The painting features a three-dimensional* ***perspective*** *view of Toronto.*

**Prospective** means likely to occur.
*The* ***prospective*** *buyer went to the company's web site to learn more.*

## Perspicacious, perspicuous

**Perspicacious** means having a quick understanding of things.
*Anand is a* ***perspicacious*** *student of law and knows the subject well.*

**Perspicuous** means expressing or presenting things clearly.
*Their account of the events is quite* ***perspicuous*** *to everyone.*

## Persuade, convince

*See entry for* ***Convince, persuade.***

## Phase, faze

*See entry for* ***Faze, phase.***

## Phenomena, phenomenon

**Phenomena** is the plural form of the noun **phenomenon**.
*Such* ***phenomena*** *are not always easy to comprehend or explain.*
*Many sightings continue to fuel the UFO* ***phenomenon.***

## Picaresque, picturesque

**Picaresque** refers to adventurers or clever rogues.
*Twain's "Tom Sawyer" contains many* ***picaresque*** *characters.*

**Picturesque** refers to being attractive or pretty.
*Lake Placid contains some of the most* ***picturesque*** *views in the state.*

## PIN number

Redundancy. **PIN** means *Personal Identification Number*. Just use **PIN**.

## Plaintiff, plaintive

**Plaintiff** refers to one who takes legal action to a court.
*She is serving notice to the **plaintiff** not to proceed with the hearing.*

**Plaintive** refers to being mournful or melancholy.
*A **plaintive** cry for help could be heard in the distance.*

## Plan on, plan to

**Plan to** is the preferred phrase.
*Please **plan to** attend our next chapter meeting.*

## Playwright, playwrite

Someone who writes plays is called a **playwright**, not a **playwrite**.

## Plenitude, plentitude

**Plenitude** is preferred in American usage.

## Plethora, dearth

*See entry for **Dearth, plethora**.*

## Plurality, majority

*See entry for **Majority, plurality**.*

## Podium, lectern

*See entry for* ***Lectern, podium.***

## Pom-pom, pompon

**Pom-pom** is an automatic weapon. **Pompon** is what a cheerleader waves.

## Populace, populous

**Populace**, a noun, refers to the common people, masses, or population.
*The city of Los Angeles has a huge and still growing* ***populace.***

**Populous**, an adjective, means densely populated.
*San Diego is a* ***populous*** *and growing southern California city.*

## Portend, pretend

**Portend** means to indicate beforehand.
*An increase in downsizing could* ***portend*** *a tough job market.*

**Pretend** means to give a false show of something.
*Just about every child likes to* ***pretend*** *sometime that they are adults.*

## Portion, apportion, proportion

*See entry for* ***Apportion, portion, proportion.***

## Possible, probable

**Possible** means something could happen but the likelihood is slim.
*It's **possible** the hurricane could hit New York by next week.*

**Probable** means something may very well happen.
*It's **probable** the hurricane hits the Carolina coast within the hour.*

## Postpone, cancel, delay

*See entry for **Cancel, delay, postpone.***

## Practicable, practical

**Practicable** means capable of being put into practice.
*Considering the financial hurdles, is it **practicable** to build a new arena?*

**Practical** means useful, sensible, or worth being put into practice.
*The action plan contains **practical** measures for improving traffic flow.*

## Pragmatic, dogmatic

*See entry for **Dogmatic, pragmatic.***

## Precede, proceed

**Precede** means to go before something.
*The National Anthem **precedes** all our baseball games.*

**Proceed** means to go ahead with an action.
*Click here if you wish to **proceed** to the next step.*

## Precedence, precedents

**Precedence** refers to priority, rank, or an act of coming before.
*The need for child safety took **precedence** over all other matters.*

**Precedents** refers to previous actions that serve as examples.
*Landmark decisions have established **precedents** for the pursuit of justice.*

## Precipitate, precipitous

**Precipitate** means rash or sudden.
*Their **precipitate** entry into the dot com market led to a disaster.*

**Precipitous** means very steep.
*Video conferencing is leading to a **precipitous** decline in travel costs.*

## Predominant, predominate

**Predominant**, an adjective, means the most common or conspicuous.
*The **predominant** view is that he is one of the best athletes in the world.*

**Predominate**, a verb, means prevail or the greater power or quantity.
*The good will of the people definitely **predominates** in this town.*
*A lack of Special Education teachers **predominates** in many states.*

Note: Older dictionaries list both words as synonyms if used as adjectives.

## Preface, foreword

*See entry for **Foreword, preface.***

## Prejudice, prejudiced

**Prejudice** is the noun and **prejudiced** is the adjective.
*Her book shows evidence of how **prejudice** is learned and unlearned.*
*We found the articles irresponsible and **prejudiced** against the groups.*

## Premature, immature

*See entry for **Immature, premature.***

## Premier, premiere

**Premier** means first in importance or chief government executive.
*That is one of the **premier** magazines on the newsstands today.*
*The **Premier** of that country invited us to his palace for dinner.*

**Premiere** means opening night or first public performance of something.
*We attended the London **premiere** of "The Phantom of the Opera".*

## Prescribe, proscribe

**Prescribe** means to set down a rule or to order.
*The labor law **prescribes** a standard 40-hour workweek.*
*Perhaps the doctor can **prescribe** a more effective drug.*

**Proscribe** means to condemn, forbid, or prohibit.
*The Food and Drug Administration **proscribed** Laetrile years ago.*

## Presentiment, presentment

**Presentiment** means premonition.
*The studio has a strong **presentiment** that the film will be a success.*

**Presentment** means something exhibited, expressed, or presented.
*Cheryl reimburses you upon* ***presentment*** *of a signed bill of exchange.*

## Press, click, type

*See entry for* ***Click, press, type.***

## Presume, assume

*See entry for* ***Assume, presume.***

## Presumptive, presumptuous

**Presumptive**, more a legal word, means not totally established.
*His refusal to submit to the test is* ***presumptive*** *evidence of use.*

**Presumptuous** means arrogant, bold, or forward.
*It is* ***presumptuous*** *of them to invite themselves to our holiday party.*

## Pretense, pretext

**Pretense** is a false claim or a show of insincere behavior.
*The drug should not be legalized, under any* ***pretense.***
*The compliments we received were all* ***pretense.***

**Pretext** is the cover up of something for a false reason.
*Mark lost his job under the* ***pretext*** *of being overqualified.*

## Preventative, preventive

**Preventive** is the preferred spelling, but either one is acceptable.
***Preventive** dentistry measures can lead to healthier smiles.*

## Principal, principle

**Principal** can be a noun or adjective that means foremost, the head of a school, or the amount of money borrowed.
*Who are the **principal** developers of the product?*
*The middle school is getting a new **principal** next year.*
*The mortgage payment includes both **principal** and interest.*

**Principle** is a noun that refers to law or personal conviction.
*It works on the **principle** that warm air rises.*
*It is against our basic **principle** to make such a statement.*

## Prodigy, protégé, protégée

**Prodigy** refers to a person with exceptional talents.
*Many musicians consider Mozart a child **prodigy**.*

**Protégé** refers to a male who is guided or helped by someone else.
*As a youth, Justin considered himself a **protégé** of Buddy Holly.*

**Protégée** refers to a female who is guided or helped by someone else.
*As a youth, Loretta considered herself a **protégée** of Patsy Cline.*

## Prognosis, diagnosis

*See entry for **Diagnosis, prognosis.***

## Prohibit, forbid

*See entry for **Forbid, prohibit.***

## Prone, prostrate, supine

**Prone** means lying face down.
*No one should move the injured player from the **prone** position.*

**Prostrate** means lying face down (often as the result of some accident).
*Last week's tornado **prostrated** many trees in the neighborhood.*

**Supine** means lying face up.
*The beach is full of sun worshippers, **supine** on the sand.*

## Proof, evidence

*See entry for **Evidence, proof.***

## Prophecy, prophesy

**Prophecy**, a noun, means a prediction.
*Is there a **prophecy** in that Psalm that could be fulfilled this year?*

**Prophesy**, a verb, means to predict by divine inspiration.
*What did they **prophesy** about our future on earth?*

## Protagonist, antagonist

*See entry for **Antagonist, protagonist.***

## Proved, proven

**Proved**, a verb, means to establish the truth of something.
*The inconsistencies in the defendant's testimony **proved** he was lying.*

**Proven**, a past participle of *prove*, is used only as an adjective.
*Hypnosis is a **proven** and popular method for quitting smoking.*

## Prudent, prudish

**Prudent** means exercising good common sense or judgment.
*It was **prudent** of Cathy and Pat to invest with the firm when they did.*

**Prudish** means very formal, precise, or reserved.
*Our company is too **prudish** to introduce a relaxed dress code.*

## PSAT test

Redundancy. **PSAT** means *Preliminary Scholastic Assessment Test.* Just use **PSAT**.

## Pseudo, quasi

**Pseudo** is a prefix meaning false, counterfeit, or deceptive. It requires a hyphen when joining proper nouns.
***Pseudo**science*
***Pseudo**-European*

**Quasi** is a prefix meaning resembling or in some manner. It is usually hyphenated.
*Quasi-scientific literature*

Note: More often now we see **pseudo** and **quasi** treated as individual words in addition to prefixes (*a **pseudo** company, a **quasi** corporation*).

## PST time

Redundancy. PST means *Pacific Standard Time.* Just use PST.

## Purposefully, purposely

**Purposefully** means to do something with determination or purpose.
*The winning coach strode **purposefully** to the TV booth for an interview.*

**Purposely** means to do something deliberately or intentionally.
*Please do not remove those books because I put them there **purposely**.*

# Q

*"One should not aim at being possible to understand, but at being impossible to misunderstand."* — Quintillian

## Qualitative, quantitative

**Qualitative** refers to the characteristics or properties of quality.
*Gerry gave the students the* ***qualitative*** *data to do the research.*

**Quantitative** refers to the quantity of something.
*The 15* ***quantitative*** *comparison questions use a different format.*

## Quasi, pseudo

*See entry for* ***Pseudo, quasi.***

## Queue, cue

*See entry for* ***Cue, queue.***

## Quiet, quite

**Quiet** means silence.
*"All* ***Quiet*** *on the Western Front" is the first antiwar film of the sound era.*

**Quite** means really.
*The banana could* ***quite*** *possibly be the world's perfect food.*

## Quotation, quote

**Quotation**, a noun, refers to words quoted or the act of quoting.
*The* ***quotations*** *of JFK and Churchill have always been very popular.*

**Quote**, a verb, means to repeat the words of someone.
*Do you mind if the press* ***quotes*** *you on that statement?*

Note: Used informally, **quote** is the shortened word for **quotation**.
*The online service offers a daily* ***quote*** *on all stock prices.*
*That movie has many memorable* ***quotes****.*

# R

*"Scarcely any of our intellectual operations could be carried on to any considerable extent without the agency of words."* — Peter Roget

## Rack, wrack

**Rack** and **wrack** both mean to strain or torment. Prefer the verb **rack**.
*We are **racking** our brains trying to remember the name of that artist.*

## RAM memory

Redundancy. **RAM** means *Random Access Memory*. Just use **RAM**.

## Rare, scarce

**Rare** means seldom seen, unusual, or uncommon.
*The **rare** recordings of Elvis are worth many dollars.*

**Scarce** means deficient, not plentiful, or small in quantity.
*The supply of electricity is **scarce** in some states.*

## Rarely ever

Avoid this phrase. Just use **rarely** by itself.
*Rarely (*not **rarely ever***) do we hire someone without a college degree.*

## Ravage, ravish

**Ravage** means to destroy or devastate something.
*Fires continued to **ravage** the western states for weeks.*

**Ravish** means to carry off by force, or overwhelm with emotion.
*She was **ravished** by her captors.*
*The beauty of the Canadian sunset **ravished** the travelers.*

## Real, really

**Real** is an adjective or adverb meaning very good.
*Patrick is a **real** friend to many people.*
*We had a **real** good time at Patrick's birthday party.*

**Really** is an adverb meaning truly or genuinely.
*We **really** had a good time at Patrick's birthday party.*

## Rebound, redound

**Rebound** means to bounce or spring back.
*The success of the company can likely **rebound** its stock price.*

**Redound** means to contribute or lead to something.
*Her exceptional performance **redounds** to the company's benefit.*

## Rebuff, rebut, refute, repudiate

**Rebuff** means to snub or reject someone.
*We offered to help with the cleanup, but they surprisingly **rebuffed** us.*

**Rebut** means to argue against someone's statement.
*Unless the defense **rebuts** it, the idea is legally accepted.*

**Refute** means to prove something is false.
*The defense team was able to **refute** much of the earlier testimony.*

**Repudiate** means to reject or refuse something.
*We were always taught to **repudiate** discrimination and violence.*

## Recapitulate, capitulate

*See entry for **Capitulate, recapitulate.***

## Recital, concert

*See entry for **Concert, recital.***

## Recur, reoccur

**Reoccur** is not a word.

## Reeking havoc, wreaking havoc

**Wreaking havoc** is the correct phrase.
*The virus is **wreaking havoc** with our new computer.*

## Refer, allude, elude

*See entry for **Allude, elude, refer.***

## Regardless, irregardless

*See entry for* ***Irregardless, regardless.***

## Regretfully, regrettably

**Regretfully** means with feelings of regret.
*Prior commitments made him* ***regretfully*** *decline the invitation.*

**Regrettably** means unfortunately.
*It looked like the rain would finally stop, but* ***regrettably*** *it did not.*

## Relegate, delegate

*See entry for* ***Delegate, relegate.***

## Reluctant, reticent

**Reluctant** means opposing or unwilling to act.
*A few golfers are* ***reluctant*** *to wear soft spikes on the course.*

**Reticent** means keeping silent or unwilling to speak freely.
*Christine's* ***reticent*** *nature conceals many of her talents and successes.*

## Remarkable, marked

*See entry for* ***Marked, remarkable.***

## Remediable, remedial

**Remediable** means capable of being corrected or remedied.
*From a practical standpoint, the defects are* ***remediable.***

**Remedial** means supplying a remedy.
*A research brief on **remedial** education is now available at the main desk.*

## Renounce, denounce

*See entry for **Denounce, renounce.***

## Repertoire, repertory

**Repertoire** is the range of entertainment a company or player performs.
*Larry has a good **repertoire** of corny jokes that we enjoy.*

**Repertory** is the place where a company or player usually performs.
*The Owego drama players now have their own **repertory** theatre.*

## Represented, representated

**Representated** is not a word.

## Reputation, character

*See entry for **Character, reputation.***

## Request, behest

*See entry for **Behest, request.***

## Respectably, respectfully, respectively

**Respectably** means in a decent way worthy of respect.
*Donna, Richard, and Dana are dressed **respectably** for the occasion.*

**Respectfully** means in a courteous way.
*Tom* ***respectfully*** *submitted his opinion to the council.*

**Respectively** means in the order given or indicated.
*Harold and Ted are an engineer and lawyer,* ***respectively.***

## Retroactive from, retroactive to

**Retroactive to** is the preferred phrase.
*The salary increases are* ***retroactive to*** *January 1.*

## Revenge, avenge

*See entry for* ***Avenge, revenge.***

## Revolve, rotate

These words are synonyms in everyday writing but not in scientific writing.
*The earth* ***revolves*** *around the sun and simultaneously* ***rotates*** *upon its axis.*

## Riffle, rifle

**Riffle** means to browse or thumb through something.
*She* ***riffled*** *the class material just before the test.*

**Rifle** means to ransack or steal something.
*Someone* ***rifled*** *through their house while they were out of town.*

## Right, wright

**Right** means morally, legally, or properly.
*Tom Hanks did the* ***right*** *thing with his film about one-hit wonders.*

**Wright** is a maker such as a playwright.
*Many people consider Neil Simon a famous American **wright**.*

## Rightfully, rightly

**Rightfully** means having a claim or right to something.
*Marty is **rightfully** the owner of the rare painting.*

**Rightly** means correctly or properly.
*Joe **rightly** refuses to sign his contract until an agreement is reached.*

## Robbery, burglary, theft

*See entry for **Burglary, robbery, theft**.*

# S

*"My words fly up, my thoughts remain below: Words without thoughts never to heaven go."* — William Shakespeare

## Sachet, sashay

**Sachet** is a small packet of perfumed powder.
*While drying her clothes, Lois dropped a small* ***sachet*** *in the dryer.*

**Sashay** means to strut or flounce.
*Beth* ***sashayed*** *proudly around the room after getting a great report card.*

## Safe-deposit box, safety deposit box

**Safe-deposit box** is the correct phrase.

## SALT talks

Redundancy. **SALT** means *Strategic Arms Limitations Talks.* Just use **SALT**.

## Sanctimony, sanctity

**Sanctimony** means pretended holiness.
*His* ***sanctimony*** *is only exceeded by his insensibility to others.*

**Sanctity** means the quality or condition of being sacred.
*Many people commit themselves to uphold the* ***sanctity*** *of life.*

## Sarcastic, skeptical, cynical

*See entry for* ***Cynical, sarcastic, skeptical.***

## SAT test

Redundancy. **SAT** means *Scholastic Assessment Test*. Just use **SAT**.

## Scarce, rare

*See entry for* ***Rare, scarce.***

## Schilling, shilling

**Schilling** is Austrian currency and **shilling** is British currency.

## Scrupulous, meticulous

*See entry for* ***Meticulous, scrupulous.***

## Scull, skull

**Scull** is an oar used by a rower.
*Dan and Ben are propelling their new canoe with heavy* ***sculls.***

**Skull** is the skeleton that protects the brain and face.
*You can get a slight* ***skull*** *fracture and sometimes not realize it.*

## Seasonable, seasonal

**Seasonable** means it is appropriate for the season or occasion.
*The sleet is unexpected but* ***seasonable*** *for this time of year.*

**Seasonal** means a particular season.
*Her **seasonal** work includes giving golf lessons in Miami.*

## Seeing as, seeing that

Avoid these phrases in writing. Use *because* instead.
***Because** our car broke down, we missed our starting time.*

## Semiannual

Synonym for *biannual* (twice a year). *See entry for **Biannual, biennial.***

## Semimonthly, bimonthly

*See entry for **Bimonthly, semimonthly.***

## Sensual, sensuous

**Sensual** means physically gratifying the body or its senses.
*She delighted in the **sensual** warmth of the Hawaiian Islands.*

**Sensuous** means appealing to the senses.
*His music is warm and **sensuous** and designed especially for relaxation.*

## Session, cession

*See entry for **Cession, session.***

## SGML language

Redundancy. **SGML** means *Standard Generalized Markup Language.* Just use **SGML**.

## Shall, will

For legal documents and some government contracts, **shall** expresses determination or a guarantee, and **will** expresses a plan to do something. Either word can be used for first, second, or third-person pronouns in the future tense.

*We (You, They)* ***shall*** *supply the required documentation when requested by the customer.*

Today in everyday American business writing and speaking, the ***wills*** out number the ***shalls***. Few people make this distinction anymore. But if you are a traditionalist, here are the rules for handling **shall** and **will**:

**Shall** is used for the first-person future tense.
*We* ***shall*** *enjoy working for the new supervisor.*

**Will** is used for the second and third-person future tense.
*You (They)* ***will*** *enjoy working for your new supervisor.*

## Shanty, chantey

*See entry for* ***Chantey, shanty.***

## Should have, should of

**Should have** is the correct phrase.
*We **should have** known it was too good to be true.*

## Shudder, shutter

**Shudder** means to shake or tremble.
*The earthquake made all the tall buildings **shudder**.*

**Shutter** is a screen or cover.
*A camera's **shutter** is similar to a person's eyelid.*

## Sight, site, cite

*See entry for **Cite, sight, site**.*

## Silicon, silicone

**Silicon** is the nonmetallic chemical element used for making microchips.
*California's Santa Clara Valley is known as the **Silicon** Valley.*

**Silicone** is plastic and other materials that contain silicon.
***Silicone** is widely used as a protective coating for shoes.*

## Simple, simplistic

**Simple** means plain, not complex, or uncomplicated.
*Joe's explanation is quite **simple** and easy to comprehend.*

**Simplistic** means unrealistically simple or oversimplified.
*Bob's explanation is quite **simplistic** and omits many key points.*

## Simulate, emulate

*See entry for* ***Emulate, simulate.***

## Sister-in-laws, sisters-in-law

**Sisters-in-law** is the correct phrase.

## Slander, liable, libel, lible

*See entry for* ***Liable, libel, lible, slander.***

## Some body, somebody

**Some body** refers to any single person or thing.
*Did you talk with* ***some body*** *in the administration about the problem?*

**Somebody** refers to any person.
***Somebody*** *can talk to the administration about the problem.*

## Some day, someday

**Some day** refers to a particular day.
*We all hope and pray that* ***some day*** *soon they are back together.*

**Someday** refers to an indefinite time in the future.
*No doubt, we'll succeed* ***someday.***

## Some one, someone

**Some one** refers to any single person or thing.
*Did you talk with* ***some one*** *in the administration about the problem?*

**Someone** refers to any person.
***Someone*** *can talk to the administration about the problem.*

## Some time, sometime, sometimes

**Some time** means a period of time.
*Gordon needs* ***some time*** *to think over the attractive job offer.*

**Sometime** refers to an indefinite time in the future.
*Let's get together and have lunch* ***sometime.***

**Sometimes** means now and then.
*James and Tim like golf a lot, but* ***sometimes*** *they need to give it a rest.*

## Somewhere, somewheres

**Somewhere** is the correct word.
*I know you're out there* ***somewhere.***

## Son-in-laws, sons-in-law

**Sons-in-law** is the correct phrase.

## Southward, southwards

**Southward** is preferred in American usage.

## Spacious, specious

**Spacious** means roomy or large in area.
*Our good friends in Clinton invited us to their* ***spacious*** *summer camp.*

**Specious** means plausible but false.
*Ted is known for using* ***specious*** *arguments in court to back his claims.*

## Spade, spayed

**Spade** refers to a small digging tool.
*The soil in our garden can be turned by hand with a* ***spade.***

**Spayed** refers to excising the ovaries of a female animal.
***Spayed*** *cats are typically affectionate, calm, and healthy.*

## Specially, especially

*See entry for* ***Especially, specially.***

## Specie, species

Concerning classification in biology, **species** is the correct spelling for both singular and plural.
*This* (or *those*) ***species*** *are soon to be extinct.*

## SPF factor

Redundancy. **SPF** means *Skin Protection Factor*. Just use **SPF**.

## Spiritual, spirituous

**Spiritual** refers to the spirit or soul.
*Friends can offer comfort, empathy, and **spiritual** support.*

**Spirituous** refers to certain kinds of alcoholic drinks.
*The license permits the sale of **spirituous** liquors in sealed containers.*

## Spoor, spore

**Spoor** is the track or trail of an animal.
*The hunters are tracking the deer by its own **spoor**.*

**Spore** is a plant's reproductive organ.
*All of these plants contain **spores**.*

## Sporadic, periodic

*See entry for **Periodic, sporadic**.*

## Stalactites, stalagmites

Both words refer to crystalline deposits of calcium carbonate found in caves. **Stalactites** hang from the ceiling, and **stalagmites** rise from the ground.

## Stanch, staunch

**Stanch** means to block something.
*Congress is allocating many dollars to **stanch** the flow of illegal drugs.*

**Staunch** means dedicated or loyal.
*Bob is always a **staunch** supporter of that political party.*

Note: **Staunch** can also mean watertight or sound (*a **staunch** ship*).

## Stationary, stationery

**Stationary** means unable to move or standing still.
***Stationary** bikes offer a great cardio lower-body workout.*

**Stationery** is paper for letter writing.
*Creating personalized business **stationery** continues to get easier.*

## Statue, stature, statute

**Statue** refers to a sculpture that represents a human or animal.
*Including the base and pedestal, the **Statue** of Liberty is 305 feet tall.*

**Stature** refers to height or status.
*The child may have a genetic short **stature** or a growth delay.*
*Their company grew in **stature** in just a few years.*

**Statute** refers to an established law or rule.
*The **statute** of limitations limits the time for tax collection activities.*

## Stimulant, stimulus

**Stimulant** refers to drugs, alcohol, and things that increase activity.
*Caffeine, a mild **stimulant,** acts on the central nervous system.*

**Stimulus** refers to an incentive that initiates activity.
*Music alone can provide a **stimulus** to the imagination.*

## Straight, strait

**Straight** means not curved.
*The Hudson River runs **straight** for almost a mile.*

**Strait** means confined, restricted, or a narrow passage.
*He is a pretty **strait**-laced type of person with high principles.*
*The **Strait** of Hormuz is the entrance to the Persian Gulf.*

## Stupid, ignorant

*See entry for **Ignorant, stupid.***

## Subnormal, abnormal

*See entry for **Abnormal, subnormal.***

## Subsequent, consequent

*See entry for **Consequent, subsequent.***

## Substantial, substantive

**Substantial** means considerable or sizeable.
*We need a **substantial** increase in revenue to meet this year's goals.*

**Substantive** means actual or firm.
*The leader is taking **substantive** measures to fight inflation.*

## Supercede, supersede

The preferred spelling is **supersede.**

## Supine, prone, prostrate

*See entry for **Prone, prostrate, supine.***

## Supplement, augment

*See entry for **Augment, supplement.***

## Suppose to, supposed to

**Supposed to** is the correct phrase.

**Suppose**, a verb, means to think or guess.
***Suppose** we win the lottery next week. What are we buying first?*

**Supposed**, an adjective, means accepted as such or believed.
*Why are we **supposed** to eat chicken soup when we are sick?*

## Sure, surely

**Sure** is an adjective that modifies nouns or pronouns.
*Waiting for hours is a **sure** sign of his patience.*

**Surely** is an adverb that modifies verbs, adjectives, and adverbs.
*Waiting for hours is **surely** a sign of his patience.*

Note: Careful writers try to avoid using the following informal uses of **sure**:
***Sure** enough, I'll be there.*
*She **sure** is a nice person.*
*He **sure** needed the money.*
***Sure**, I want to attend college.*

## Sure and, sure to

**Sure to** is the correct phrase.
*Be **sure to** negotiate beneficial compromises for all your clients.*

## SUV vehicle

Redundancy. **SUV** means *Sport Utility Vehicle*. Just use **SUV**.

## Sympathy, empathy

*See entry for **Empathy, sympathy**.*

## Syntax, grammar

*See entry for **Grammar, syntax**.*

## Systematize, systemize

**Systematize** is the preferred spelling, but either one is acceptable.

# T

*"Use the right word and not its second cousin."* — Mark Twain

## T–shirt, tee shirt

Either spelling is acceptable.

## Take, bring

*See entry for **Bring, take.***

## Take a different tack, take a different tact

**Take a different tack** is the correct phrase (meaning to turn).
*We are going **to take a different tack** this semester and focus on math.*

## Tantamount, paramount

*See entry for **Paramount, tantamount.***

## Taunt, taut

**Taunt** means to jeer, mock, scoff, or tease someone.
*Ed plans on confronting the person who **taunted** him during his speech.*

**Taut** means tightly stretched or tense.
*The rope has to be kept **taut** for the rock climb.*

## Teach, learn

*See entry for* ***Learn, teach.***

## Temerity, timidity

**Temerity** means daring or reckless.
*Nick had the* ***temerity*** *to ask the celebrity for two more autographs.*

**Timidity** means fearful or hesitant.
*The child has the* ***timidity*** *and shyness common to many young children.*

## Temperature, fever

*See entry for* ***Fever, temperature.***

## Tenant, tenet

**Tenant** refers to one who holds the right (or lease) to occupy a place.
*The previous* ***tenant*** *of this house lived here for 7 years.*

**Tenet** refers to a rule, belief, or part of a body of doctrine.
*Avoiding pork is a* ***tenet*** *of some faiths.*

## That there, them there, these here, this here

Avoid these phrases. Just use ***that***, ***those***, ***these***, or ***this***.

## That, which

**That** is used when the word introduces a clause essential (or restrictive) to the meaning of the sentence. **That** helps identify the information and is not set off by commas.

*This is the Chevy* **that** *is 5 years old.*
*Here is the rule* **that** *applies in both cases.*

**Which** is used when the word introduces a clause not essential (or non-restrictive) to the meaning of the sentence. **Which** helps amplify the information and is set off by commas or other punctuation.

*My Chevy,* ***which*** *runs well, is 5 years old.*
*This rule,* ***which*** *became effective in 2002, applies in both cases.*

Memory hook: **That** identifies and **which** amplifies.

## Their, there, they're

**Their** is the possessive of the pronoun *they*; **there** is an adverb or a pronoun referring to a place; **they're** is the contraction of *they are.*
***They're*** *doing all* ***their*** *homework over* ***there*** *tonight.*

## Theirself, theirselves, themself

No such words exist. Substitute *herself* or *himself* for **theirself** and *themselves* for **theirselves** and **themself.**

## Thence, hence, whence

*See entry for* ***Hence, thence, whence.***

## Therefor, therefore

**Therefor** means for this or for that.
*He is actually working at various jobs and being paid* ***therefor.***

**Therefore** means hence or consequently.
*We **therefore** hold that the 2-week notice adequately informs them.*

## These kind, those kind

Avoid these phrases because you are mixing a plural word (*these* or *those*) with a singular word (*kind*). Instead, use *this kind* and *that kind*, or *these kinds* and *those kinds.*

Note that this agreement problem can also occur with the phrases *these sort* and *these type.*

## These ones, those ones

Avoid these phrases. Just use **these** or **those** without the word **ones.**

## Thrash, thresh

**Thrash** means to beat, defeat, or move violently.
*In last week's game we **thrashed** the opposition.*
*People in the exercise class **thrashed** their arms about like windmills.*

**Thresh** means to separate seeds of cereal from husks by beating.
*The workers **thresh** the wheat in the fields weekly.*

## Throughway, thruway

**Thruway**, meaning an expressway, is the more common word. It is derived from the words *through* and *highway.*

## Thru, through

Though it is quite common, **thru** is a nonstandard word and should be avoided. Use **through** instead.

## Thus, thusly

**Thusly** is a nonstandard word. Avoid its use.

## Tidbit, titbit

**Tidbit** is preferred in American usage.

## Till, until

Though considered less formal, the word **till** is acceptable shorthand for **until**. Also, many people prefer starting a sentence with **until** rather than **till**.

Note that **'til**, a contraction of **until**, is an old form that has been replaced by **till**.

## Tint, hue, shade

*See entry for **Hue, shade, tint.***

## Titillate, titivate

**Titillate** means to stimulate, tickle, or arouse pleasantly.
*The specially prepared Buffalo chicken wings **titillate** our taste buds.*

**Titivate** means adorned, spruced up, or tidy.
*Hand-painted murals of famous jazz musicians* ***titivate*** *the walls.*

## Titled, entitled

*See entry for* ***Entitled, titled.***

## Tongue and cheek, tongue in cheek

**Tongue in cheek** is the correct phrase (meaning usually kidding).
*Kim wrote a lighthearted* ***tongue in cheek*** *article about his hometown.*

## Tortuous, torturous

**Tortuous** means winding or crooked.
*The bus took a* ***tortuous*** *route getting to the concert venue.*

**Torturous** means causing pain or torture.
*The steep mountain path is quite* ***torturous*** *to our legs and feet.*

## Toward, towards

**Toward** is preferred in American usage.

## Track home, tract home

**Tract home** is the correct phrase. It refers to a mass-produced house that has a common construction method and design.
***Tract homes*** *continue to be popular in many areas of the U.S.*

## Transient, transitory

**Transient** means temporary, brief, or fleeting; it usually applies to people.
*Mr. Dracon and Mr. Sasnowitz are **transient** guests at this hotel.*

**Transitory** means the same as **transient**, but it usually applies to events.
*By being on the road, the two engineers are in a **transitory** situation.*

## Translucent, transparent, opaque

*See entry for **Opaque, translucent, transparent.***

## Triumphal, triumphant

**Triumphal** means to celebrate or honor a success or victory.
*The baseball team had a **triumphal** celebration in their home city.*

**Triumphant** means to show a feeling of rejoice for success or victory.
*The crowd is greeting the players with **triumphant** shouts of joy.*

## Troop, troupe

**Troop** is a group of people or animals.
*A **troop** of freshman college students are attending orientation week.*

**Troupe** is a company of actors or performers.
*The Ithaca College Trombone **Troupe** was formally started in 1982.*

## Trustee, trusty

**Trustee** is someone who is entrusted to manage the property of others.
*Mary Jane is the public guardian and **trustee** of their estate.*

**Trusty** is a trustworthy prisoner who has special privileges.
*The dependable **trusty** was given a new job in the prison's library.*

## Try and, try to

**Try to** remember that **try to** is the correct phrase.
*We **try to** negotiate beneficial compromises for all our clients.*

## Turbid, turgid

**Turbid** means muddy, opaque, or unclear.
*The mountain lake appears **turbid** after the rainfall.*

**Turgid** means swollen or pompous.
*Steve's abdominal area is **turgid** from the surgery.*
*The radio personality has a **turgid** style of talking.*

## Turn into, turn to

**Turn into** means to transform.
*Contrary to popular belief, muscles never **turn into** fat.*

**Turn to** means seek advice or solace from, or go to a particular place.
*Dissatisfied with his golf scores, Bill **turned to** his pro for advice.*
*The professor asked the class to please **turn to** page 100.*

## Typhoon, hurricane

*See entry for **Hurricane, typhoon.***

# U

*"Writers take words seriously - perhaps the last professional class that does."*
— John Updike

## Ultimate, penultimate

*See entry for* ***Penultimate, ultimate.***

## Unalienable, inalienable

Either word is correct, but **inalienable** is more common today.

## Unaware, unawares

**Unaware** is an adjective that means not being aware of something.
*The organizers are* ***unaware*** *of the bad weather that is forecast.*

**Unawares** is an adverb meaning by surprise or unexpectedly.
*The bad weather caught the picnic organizers* ***unawares.***

## Unbeknown, unbeknownst

Either spelling is acceptable.

## Unbelievable

This is a much overused word. It actually means too *improbable to believe* rather than its misuse of *good.*

*Mary makes* **good** *(not* **unbelievable***) apple pies every fall.*
*To some, the famous UFO story of Roswell, New Mexico is* **unbelievable.**

## Under way, underway

Either spelling is acceptable.

## Undoubtably, undoubtedly

**Undoubtably** is not a word.

## Unequivocably, unequivocally

**Unequivocably** is not a word.

## Unhealthful, unhealthy

*See entry for* ***Healthful, healthy.***

## Uninterested, disinterested

*See entry for* ***Disinterested, uninterested.***

## Unorganized, disorganized

*See entry for* ***Disorganized, unorganized.***

## Unreadable, illegible

*See entry for* ***Illegible, unreadable.***

## Unsatisfied, dissatisfied

*See entry for **Dissatisfied, unsatisfied.***

## Until, till

Though considered less formal, the word **till** is acceptable shorthand for **until**. Also, many people prefer starting a sentence with **until** rather than **till**.

Note that **'til**, a contraction of **until**, is an old form that has been replaced by **till**.

## Unwanted, unwonted

**Unwanted** means not wanted.
*The dog is **unwanted** and abandoned, yet beautiful and friendly.*

**Unwonted** means out of the ordinary or unusual.
*At the party, the children were in an **unwonted** state of excitement.*

## UPC code

Redundancy. **UPC** means *Universal Product Code*. Just use **UPC**.

## Upward, upwards

**Upward** is preferred in American usage.

## Urban, urbane

**Urban** refers to a city.
*A good example of continued **urban** sprawl is Las Vegas, Nevada.*

**Urbane** means polished or smooth.
*The diplomat's **urbane** manner impresses everyone.*

## Use to, used to

**Used to** is the correct phrase.
*We **used to** listen to their music all the time.*

## Utmost, outmost

*See entry for **Outmost, utmost.***

# V

*"I know many books which have bored their readers, but I know of none which has done real evil."* — Voltaire

## Varied, various

**Varied** means altered or changed.
*The test questions **varied** from general to specific subjects.*

**Various** means distinct, diverse, or many different kinds.
*The company officers come from **various** technical backgrounds.*

## VAT tax

Redundancy. **VAT** means *Value Added Tax*. Just use **VAT**.

## Venal, venial

**Venal** means susceptible to corruption, dishonesty, or bribery.
*The candidate did not commit the **venal** offense of bribing voters.*

**Venial** means easily excused or forgiven.
*Eating meat on Fridays was once a **venial** sin in the Catholic religion.*

## Veracious, voracious

**Veracious** means completely truthful or accurate.
*When the **veracious** child speaks, never doubt the accuracy of her story.*

**Voracious** means having an insatiable appetite for an activity or food.
*Since he was a child, Tim has been a* ***voracious*** *reader of science fiction.*
*The appetite for fiber today is* ***voracious.***

## Verbal, oral

*See entry for* ***Oral, verbal.***

## Vicious circle, vicious cycle

**Vicious circle** is the correct phrase.
*He went through a* ***vicious circle*** *of changing jobs.*

## Villain, villein

**Villain** is a bad person.
*Every James Bond film has at least one* ***villain*** *for 007 to catch.*

**Villein** was a feudal serf in medieval Europe.
***Villeins*** *are frequently mentioned in the Domesday Book.*

## VIN number

Redundancy. **VIN** means *Vehicle Identification Number*. Just use **VIN.**

## Visa, passport

*See entry for* ***Passport, visa.***

## Vocation, avocation

*See entry for* ***Avocation, vocation.***

## Vouch, avow

*See entry for* ***Avow, vouch.***

# W

*"A new word is like a wild animal you have caught. You must learn its ways and break it before you can use it."* — H.G. Wells

## Wangle, wrangle

**Wangle** means to gain by trickery or contrivance.
*He **wangled** a position in the company for which he had no background.*

**Wrangle** means to argue or debate something quite angrily.
*The two coaches **wrangled** on many calls made by the umpire.*

**Wrangle** also relates to herding or tending saddle horses.
*Paul has been roping and **wrangling** horses in Virginia for years now.*

## Warrantee, warranty

**Warrantee** is the person to whom the **warranty** is given.
*The dealer gave the **warrantee** the required forms to complete.*

**Warranty** means an official authorization or sanction.
*Vehicles under a factory **warranty** can qualify for an extended contract.*

## Wary, weary

**Wary** means cautious or watchful.
*Beth and John are **wary** about replacing their old insurance policy.*

**Weary** means fatigued or tired.
*The players are* ***weary*** *after a long week of overtime matches.*

## Wean, ween

**Wean** means to cause to give up something.
*The doctor and I are trying to* ***wean*** *him from his daily cigarettes.*

**Ween** means to think, suppose, or imagine something.
*We are asking every student to* ***ween*** *new ideas for the school play.*

## Well, good

*See entry for* ***Good, well.***

## Went, gone

*See entry for* ***Gone, went.***

## We're, were

**We're** is a contraction for *we are.*
***We're*** *always glad to help people in need.*

**Were** is a past tense form of the verb *be.*
*Bill and Tom* ***were*** *applying to many colleges on the west coast.*

## Westward, westwards

**Westward** is preferred in American usage.

## Wet your appetite, whet your appetite

**Whet your appetite** (from *whetstone*) is correct. It means to sharpen your appetite.
*We realize the menu selection and the price **whet your appetite.***

## Whence, thence, hence

*See entry for **Hence, thence, whence.***

## Whereas, although

*See entry for **Although, whereas.***

## Which, that

*See entry for **That, which.***

## Whither, wither

**Whither** means to what place, result, or condition.
"***Whither** thou goest, I will go.*" (Ruth 1:16)

**Wither** means to dry up or shrivel from lack of moisture.
*The plants in the green house **wither** without water.*

## Who, whom

Though many people today use these words interchangeably, careful writers and speakers retain this distinction of nominative and objective pronoun case.

To choose the correct pronoun of **who** or **whom**, you need to recognize whether the pronoun is being used as a subject (the nominative form) or an object (the objective form). **Who** is nominative (for subjects), and **whom** is objective (for objects).

***Who*** *(subject) left the party last?*
***Whom*** *(object) should the invitation go to?*

Trick example:
*The gift must be returned by* ***whoever*** *bought it.*

Here the whole clause ***whoever*** *bought it* is the object of the preposition *by.* But ***whoever*** remains nominative because it is the subject of that clause.

Another tip is to try substituting a personal pronoun (*he, she, him, her, they, them,* and others) in place of **who** or **whom**. If *he, she,* or *they* fits, use **who**.

**Who** is the junior Senator from that state?
*She* is the junior Senator from that state.

If *him, her,* or *them* fits, use **whom**.

The outcome could depend on **whom**.
The outcome could depend on *them.*

## Who's, whose

**Who's** is the contraction for *who is.*
***Who's*** *that person you are recommending for the job?*

**Who's** can also mean *who has.*
***Who's** been sending money to the church anonymously?*

**Whose** is the possessive form of *who.*
***Whose** report card shows the most improvement?*

## Will, shall

*See entry for* ***Shall, will.***

## With regard to, with regards to

**With regard to**, without an *s*, is the correct phrase. Note that sometimes you can avoid this phrase and substitute words such as *on*, *about*, or *concerning.*
*He notified everyone* ***with regard to*** *(on, about, concerning) the time change.*

## Would have, would of

**Would have** is the correct phrase.
*If you had read the book, you* ***would have*** *known the correct answer.*

## Wrack, rack

*See entry for* ***Rack, wrack.***

## Wreak, wreck

**Wreak** means to cause trouble.
*Unexpected expense* ***wreaks*** *havoc on this year's budget.*

**Wreck** means to destroy.
*Unexpected expense* ***wrecked*** *our budget last year.*

## Wreaking havoc, reeking havoc

**Wreaking havoc** is the correct phrase.
*The bad weather is **wreaking havoc** on some states*

## Wreath, wreathe

**Wreath** refers to flowers or other things intertwined into a circle.
*Pat and Russ chose a colorful holiday **wreath** for the centerpiece.*

**Wreathe** means to move or proceed on a repeatedly curving course.
*The smoke continues to **wreathe** upward throughout the city.*

## Wright, right

*See entry for **Right, wright.***

# Y

*"Think like a wise man but communicate in the language of the people."*
— William Butler Yeats

## Yoke, yolk

**Yoke** means a crosspiece holding two things together.
*The oxen pulling the plow has an ancient wooden **yoke** around its neck.*

**Yolk** means a yellow part of an egg.
*The **yolk** of the egg contains most of the protein.*

## Your, you're

**Your** is the possessive form of *you*.
*It's on **your** desk.*

**You're** is a contraction of *you are*.
***You're** a winner.*

# About the Author

Dave Dowling has spent over 25 years in industry as a technical writer, editor, and instructor. His experience includes commercial and government work for IBM and Lockheed Martin.

Before a career in technical communications, Dave worked in radio syndication in Los Angeles, where he assisted in the production of nationally syndicated radio shows *American Top 40* and *American Country Countdown*. Today he is president of *Write On Course, LLC* (www.writeoncourse.com), a company that offers business and technical writing seminars throughout the U.S. In addition to being a member of the *Society for Technical Communication*, Dave is a contributing writer to the *Steve Reeves International Society* (www.stevereeves.com) in Malibu, California.

The author holds an M.S. from the State University at Albany, N.Y. and a B.A. from the State University College at Potsdam, N.Y. He currently lives in Owego, New York with his wife Mary and son Tim.

# Bibliography

The following *excellent* writing books were consulted in preparing this book:

*The Careful Writer: A Modern Guide to English Usage*, Theodore M. Bernstein. New York: Atheneum, 1977.

*College English and Communication*, Marie M. Stewart and Kenneth Zimmer. 4th ed. New York: McGraw-Hill, 1982.

*The Columbia Guide to Standard American English*, Kenneth G. Wilson. New York: Columbia University Press, 1993.

*The Elements of Style*, William Strunk Jr., and E.B. White. 3rd ed. New York: Macmillan, 1979.

*Good Grammar Made Easy*, Martin Steinmann and Michael Keller. New York: Gramercy Books, 1999.

*The Handbook of Good English*, Edward D. Johnson. New York: Facts On File Publications, 1982.

*Handbook for Writers*, Celia Millward. New York: Holt, Rinehart and Winston, 1983.

*Harbrace College Handbook*, John C. Hodges, Mary E. Whittens, Winifred B. Horner, Suzanne S. Webb, Robert K. Miller. 11th ed. New York: Harcourt Brace Jovanovich, Publishers, 1990.

*The Little, Brown Handbook*, H. Ramsey Fowler. Boston: Little, Brown and Company, 1980.

*The Office Guide to Modern English Usage*, Carol M. Barnum and Jean C. Vermes. 2nd ed. New York: MJF Books, 1991.

*Put It in Writing!*, Albert Joseph. New and Updated Edition. New York: McGraw-Hill, 1998.

*The Random House Handbook*, Frederick Crews. 3rd ed. New York: Random House, 1980.

*Sleeping Dogs Don't Lay*, Richard Lederer and Richard Dowis. New York: St. Martin's Press, 1999.

*Strictly Speaking*, Edwin Newman. New York: Warner Books, 1974.

*Woe Is I*, Patricia T. O'Conner. New York: Riverhead Books, August 1998.

*The Wordwatcher's Guide to Good Writing & Grammar*, Morton S. Freeman. Cincinnati: Writer's Digest Books, 1990.

*The Write Way*, Richard Lederer and Richard Dowis. New York: Pocket Books, 1995.

*The Writer's Art*, James J. Kilpatrick. Kansas City: Andrews and McMeel, June 1993.

The following *excellent* dictionaries and style guides were consulted in preparing this book:

*American Century Dictionary*. New York: Oxford University Press, 1997.

*American Heritage Dictionary of the English Language*. 4th ed. New York: Dell Publishing, 2000.

*Associated Press Stylebook and Libel Manual*. 6th Trade ed. New York: Addison Wesley, 1996.

*Chicago Manual of Style*. 14th ed. Chicago: Univ. of Chicago Press, 1999.

*Merriam-Webster's Collegiate Dictionary*. 10th ed. Springfield, MA: Merriam-Webster, 1996.

*Oxford American Desk Dictionary and Thesaurus*. 2nd ed. New York: Oxford University Press, 2000.

*Random House Webster's College Dictionary*. New York: Random House, 1996.

*Webster's New World College Dictionary*. 10th ed. New York: Macmillan, 1996.

*Webster's New World Roget's Thesaurus A-Z*. New York: Macmillan USA, 1999.

0-595-20830-4

Printed in the United States
6849

9 780595 208302